Design Collection with
Limited Colors

限られた色数の印刷とは単に印刷コストを低減するための手法ではなく、
微妙な色味を再現する高度なデザイン・印刷テクニックとして多用されている。
本書では、そのテクニックを用いた世界各国の作品を紹介している。
その作品から刺激を受けて、限られた色数の印刷による多様なデザイン、印刷効果の探求に挑戦されることを期待する。

Design Collection with Limited Colors is not just a way to cut down the cost of printing,
but is a high standard in design and printing technique to express the delicate color tones.
We have gathered one of the most elite design works that use this technique.
By looking at the works to be introduced, we hope they will encourage you to take a
step in trying new designs and printing in limited color.

PIE
BOOKS

Design Collection with Limited Colors

PIE BOOKS

2-32-4, Minami-Otsuka, Toshima-ku, Tokyo 170-0005 Japan
Tel: +81-3-5395-4811   Fax: +81-3-5395-4812
e-mail: editor@piebooks.com (editor office)
: sales@piebooks.com (sales division office)

ISBN978-4-89444-712-7 C3070
Printed in Japan

本書は好評につき完売した「限られた色のデザインアイデア」の改訂版です。
序文は上記タイトルのために書かれたものをそのまま使用しています。

This book was previously published in a popular hardcover edition entitled
"Design Idea with Limited Color".
References to the title in the foreword of hence reflect the original title.

CONTENTS 目次

特集：色の選択、色のイメージ

Special Articles on Choosing the Colors and Image of Colors

限られた色数の印刷の最大の難関、と同時に最大の利点となってくるのが、使用する色の選択となってくる。掛け合わせにはない、はっきりとした色を使用できるということは、その色の持つイメージを最大限に利用できるということであり、色が選択された時点で、デザインが表現しなければいけない方向性も決定してくるのだ。つまり限られた色数の印刷のデザインとは、具体的作業以前の、色の選択、イメージの把握という段階から始まっているのである。ここでは、色の選択という作業の行程ついて説明していく。また、その行程の重要な要素である色のイメージについても説明していく。このページ以降の掲載作品を見ていただくときに、そのデザイン作業の裏側に存在する色の選択という行程を想像していただくのに、また自身の作業において利用していただければと思う。

色の選択とは・・・その作業行程

最初にイメージを具体化することから始まり、それを視覚化するためのイメージ言語（視覚言語）を選ぶことになる。これには視覚化しやすい言葉（日常生活での形容詞にあたる）が選ばれることになる。イメージ言語が選択されると、そのイメージを表現できるとされる色につながることとなる。ただし、このイメージと色とのつながりには、その国々の文化、宗教、伝統、思想、習慣が密接に関係しているため、東西南北では色彩文化に差異が存在していることも事実である。ただ、その状況を踏まえた上で、以下に色についてどのようなイメージが存在するかを列挙した。掲載作品の色とイメージとの関連性を探究するのに利用していただければと思う。

色とイメージ

一つの色を見たときや色名を聞いたとき、好きとか嫌い、嬉しいとか悲しいなどの感情を伴ったイメージを心に描く。それを色の感情効果と言う。特に、男女差・老若を問わず共通する感情をその色に対する固有感情と言う。この固有感情は最も色の選択をしていく上で重要な要素となってくる。大きな分類をしていくと以下の表現が利用される。

1 暖かい色・冷たい色

赤から橙・黄までの色は、暖かく感じる色で、暖色系という。また、青緑から青・青紫までの色は、冷たく感じたり、寒く感じることから寒色系という。暖かくも寒くも感じない中間の感じ方をする黄緑・緑、紫から赤紫までの色を、中間色という。

2 軽い色・重たい色

色の軽・重感は、色の明るさに関係している。例えば、日常持っているカバンを軽快な感じにしたいときは明るく薄い色にすればよく、黒やダークブルー・紫などにすると重々しくなる。

3 派手な色・地味な色

派手・地味な感じは、彩度に関係している。鮮やかな赤・鮮やかな黄・明るい青・明るい紫で配色された着物は華やかな感じになり、逆にグレイやグレイがかった灰みの色は地味な感じになる。

Choosing the color is the most important and hardest task in design using limited color. Idea of using more vivid color can become a chance of using the image power of the color to it's full. When the color is choose, it can be said that the direction of the design will be determined also. The design ideas using limited color starts from the time of choosing the colors, and understanding the exact image of the work purpose. We will begin this book by understanding the work process of choosing the colors. And also will look at the important element of color choosing, the image of colors. By starting with this page, we hope it will help you in understanding the design backgrounds of each introduced works.

Choosing the colors····It's work process

The whole process begins with putting the image into a concrete shape, then choosing the word that would visualize the image. This word must be easy enough that we can find and use in our ordinary life. By choosing the word, it leads us to a specific color that would express the exact image. Although many of the times, this specific color can differ among countries for cultural, religious, etc. reasons. There is different color mind culture between east and west civilization. Keeping that in mind, we have introduced many of the connection between color and it's image. We hope this will help you in finding the relation between the color and image of work you will be seeing in this book.

Image and effect of colors

Colors may generate various effects according to their usage. Let's consider these psychological effects.

1. Warm colors and cool colors

Warm colors are those in the family of red, orange, and yellow, colors that make us feel warm, and remind us of the sun and fire. Cool colors are those between blue and blue-green that remind us of ice and water. Neutral colors are those in the family of green and violet that don't evoke a feeling of warmth or coolness. Warm colors can accelerate the passage of time. But cool colors can slow down the passage of time. There are also differences in the psychological temperature between warm colors and cool colors.

2. Light colors and heavy colors

Low value colors give a heavy feeling. High value (low chroma) colors impart a feeling of lightness. In general, black is the heaviest, and white is the lightest.

3. Showy colors and sober colors

Showy colors have high value and chroma, and can be efficiently combined when using many colors. In a two-color scheme, colors with large differences in hue and value look showy. Low-value and low-chroma colors give an impression of soberness.

4. Invigorating colors and soothing colors

Invigorating colors are those that give a the strong stimulus. They belong to the family of warm colors, corresponding to the high-chroma colors. Soothing colors are those that calm our heart and feeling. They belong to the family of cool colors and green, corresponding to the low-value and low-chroma colors. Colors existing in nature are organic and soothing colors.

5. Advancing colors and retreating colors

Advancing colors are those in the family of warm colors that seem to advance when high-value and high-chroma colors are used. Retreating colors are those in the family of cool colors that seem to retreat when low-value and low-chroma colors are used. Advancing colors are also called swelling colors, because they appear to be swelling. Retreating colors are also called shrinking colors because they appear to be shrinking.

Images of Typical Color

RED

Red is the warm color that is felt to be the hottest, the color of energy and abundant power. Red is one of the colors that Japanese women are fond of. Among the similar red colors, the Japanese prefer vermilion, and the Chinese, crimson. In Europe, red is magenta (a red-violet).
—— Impressions of the color red:
power of life, energy, passion, excitement, joy, vitality, anger, dissatisfaction, madness, violent emotion, danger, jealousy, cupidity, dispute, revolution, stress, oppression, frustration, aggressive, impulsive, oversensitive.
—— Physiological and psychological effects of the color red:
Increases the heart rate. Improves the secretion of adrenaline. Accelerates the metabolism. Stimulates the autonomic nerve, and heightens tension. Increases the appetite. Cheers and invigorates. Makes one feel affection, tenderness, and warmth, and relaxes. Effective for patients with autism. Awakens and excites. Seems to slow the passage of time.

YELLOW

Yellow is psychologically the color of presumption upon the love of another, dependence, and courting. Adults who like this color may be regarded as childish. According to the Japan Industrial Standards (JIS), yellow is the color designated to indicate warnings. In Japan, yellow and black stripes are used for railroad crossing to attract attention.
—— Impressions of the color yellow:
hope, happiness, bright, agile, joyful, cheerful, curious, knowledge, wisdom, pursuit, creative, openness, warning, caution, danger, haste, anxiety
—— Physiological and psychological effects of the color yellow:
Hallucinogenic effect: yellow stimulates the nerves and is effective for sufferers of melancholy and nervous breakdowns. Stimulates lymph gland secretions and improves their functions. Improves the function of the digestive system, and is effective for indigestion, gastritis, diabetes. Seems to slow the passage of time. Gives an appearance of lightness. Improves short-term mental concentration. But, if overused, may cause distraction. Stimulates primitive instincts, warns and increases awareness of danger.

4 硬い色・柔らかい色

硬い・柔らかいの感じは、軽い・柔らかいに感じと同様に明度に関係している。お菓子のクリームがかった色や、赤ちゃんの肌色を見ると柔らかい感じがする。また、チョコレートの色は硬い感じがする。

5 これらの他にも、『強・弱感』、『陽・陰感』、『興奮・鎮静感』、『明・暗感』、『澄・濁感』、『男性的・女性的』などの感情効果がある。

代表的色のイメージ

赤

赤は一番熱く感じる色（暖色）で、力があふれ出ようとするエネルギーの色。日本の女性が好む色のひとつが赤色と言われる。同じ赤色でも日本人は朱赤を、中国人は真っ赤を好む。ヨーロッパで赤といえばマゼンタ（赤紫）になる。
—— 赤色がもつイメージ
生命力、エネルギー、情熱、興奮、歓喜、元気、怒り、不満、狂気、激情、危険、嫉妬、貪欲、争い、革命、ストレス、圧迫感、欲求不満、攻撃的、衝動的、神経過敏
—— 赤色が及ぼす生理作用や心理作用
心拍数を上げる。アドレナリンの分泌をよくする。新陳代謝を促進する。自律神経を刺激し、緊張状態にする。食欲増進。人を元気づけ、より活発にさせる。愛情、優しさ、ぬくもりを感じさせ、心を和ませる。自閉症患者に効果的。覚醒、興奮状態を作り出す。時間経過を遅く感じさせる。

黄

黄色は色彩心理学的にいえば「甘え、依存、求愛」の色。幼児が好む色であることから、大人がこの色を好むと、子供っぽいイメージに見られる。また、日本工業規格には「注意」を表示する色と決められている。特に踏み切りなどに用いられる。「黒と黄」のストライプは人の目を非常に引きつけやすいのだ。
—— 黄色がもつイメージ
希望、幸福、明るい、軽快、愉快、明朗、好奇心、知識、知恵、探求、クリエイティブ、開放感、注意、警告、危険、軽率、不安
—— 黄色が及ぼす生理作用や心理作用
幻覚作用：神経を興奮させ、うつや精神の衰弱に効果がある。リンパ腺分泌系を刺激し、機能を高める。消化器系の働きを促進して消化不良、胃炎、糖尿病などによい。時間の経過を遅く感じさせる。見かけより軽く感じさせる。短時間の精神集中を促すが、使いすぎると気が散りやすくなる。原始的本能を刺激して危険を感じさせ、注意を感じさせる。

緑

安全を表し、安心感を与えてくれる色。草食動物などはライオンなどの猛獣から身を隠す茂みの色になる。激しい赤と優雅な紫の中間にあって、穏やかで安らいだ気分と結びつく。地球の大地を覆う緑は母なる大地であり、自然界の色彩の母とも呼ばれる。同じ緑でも日本の緑は黄みがかっていて、ヨーロッパの緑は青みがかっている。
—— 緑がもつイメージ
落ち着き、くつろぎ、安全、平和、安息、平等、永久、公平、慰安、親愛、安易、新鮮、自然、健康、さわやか、栄養、豊か、青春、成長、未熟、青二才
—— 緑が及ぼす生理作用や心理作用
神経系統の鎮静作用、鎮痛作用、緊張緩和、催眠作用。ストレスの減少。解毒、殺菌作用、フィトンチッドの効果＝森林浴。目を休める。食べ物の緑は人間の体を弱アルカリ性に保つ働きがある。

青

　青は世界中で一番好まれる色。日本人は川の水の色として。ヨーロッパ人は地中海、空の色として。アメリカ人は空の色として。最も平和で穏やかな色。人間が地球上に出現して以来、最も一般的な環境色としておのずと人間の情緒を規定し、育成してきた。青は後退色、収縮色の代表選手→消極的、内向的ととらえられます。

── 青が持つイメージ

知性、理性、精神、静寂、冷静、平和、清潔、気品、威厳、自制心、自律、成功、安全、信頼、瞑想、誠意、保守的、冷たい、涼しい、爽やか、堅い、広大、無限、孤独、悲しみ、冷淡、失望、憂鬱、淋しい、不安、未熟、消極的、内向的、服従、冷酷

── 青が及ぼす生理作用や心理作用

精神を沈静化させ、安定させる作用がある。集中力を促進させる。解毒、殺菌作用がある。催眠効果がある。鎮痛効果もある。内分泌系の働きを鎮静させる。発汗を押さえる作用もある。血液を浄化させたり、また、止血作用もある。新生児の黄疸症状に青の色光を当てる。

紫

　赤と青の混色によってできる色が紫。紫は高貴な色、貴重な色として存在している。日本の紫は青紫（バイオレット[violet]）（紫根染＝古代紫＝薬草＝珍重＝高貴な人＝禁色）。紫は中性色と呼ばれる。赤紫＝パープル→暖色、興奮色、進出色。青紫＝バイオレット→寒色、鎮静色、後退色。

── 紫がもつイメージ

上品、神秘的、神聖、権威、芸術的、想像力、尊厳、不安、孤独、情緒不安定、うぬぼれ

── 紫が及ぼす生理作用や心理作用

血圧、脈拍を低下させる。紫には催眠効果がある。想像力、創造力を促進させる。（＋イメージ）不安、ストレスを蓄積させる。（－イメージ）治癒効果をもっている。人体中の光回復酵素を刺激し、活動力が再び上昇する。（＋イメージ）孤独感を感じさせる。（－イメージ）

黒、白（無色）

　光をすべて吸収すると黒になる。光をすべて反射すると白になる。黒と白を混ぜると灰色になる。

日本の古語では、クロ（暗）⟷アカ（明）　明度、シロ（顕）⟷アオ（漠）　彩度。白・灰・黒のように、色味を全くもたない色を「無彩色」という。逆に少しでも色味をもっていればそれは「有彩色」という。

── 無彩色が持つイメージ

黒：負け、悪魔、マイナス、不吉、恐怖、抑圧、コンプレックス、絶望

白：勝ち、純潔、清潔、善良、真実、冷たさ、警戒心、失敗感、孤独

灰：無気力、迷い、諦め、複雑、無、不安、絶望感

GREEN

　Green is the color that expresses safety and gives a sense of security. Green is positioned between violent red and elegant violet, and is related to a calm and peaceful feeling. Among the similar greens, Japanese green is tinged with yellow, and European green is tinged with blue.

── Impressions of the color green:

serenity, relaxation, safety, peace, rest, equality, eternity, fairness, consolation, love, easygoing nature, freshness, nature, health, refreshing, nutrition, richness, adolescence, growth, immaturity, youth

── Physiological and psychological effects of the color green:

Soothing to the nervous system, pain-killing effect, relaxes tension, hypnotic effect. Decreases stress. Cleansing and sterilizing effect, purifying effect = a bath in the woods. Restful to the eyes, relaxation.

BLUE

　Blue is the color that is most loved throughout the world. Japanese recognize blue as the color of water in rivers. Europeans recognize blue as the color of the sky of Cote dAzur in the Mediterranean. Americans recognize blue as sky blue. Blue is the most peaceful and calming color. Since the appearance of humans on the Earth, blue has determined and fostered human emotion as the fundamental color of the environment. Blue is a typical retreating and shrinking color. -> It is considered to have a negative and introvertive image.

── Impressions of the color blue:

intelligence, reason, spirit, silence, calmness, peace, cleanliness, grace, dignity, self-control, independence, success, safety, trust, meditation, sincerity, conservative, cool, cool, fresh, solid, vast, infinite, solitude, sadness, coolness, disappointment, melancholy, lonely, anxiety, immaturity, negative, introvertive, obedience, cruelty

── Physiological and psychological effects of the color blue:

Soothes and stabilizes the mind. Increases the power of concentration. Cleansing and sterilizing effect. Hypnotic effect. Pain-killing effect. Calms the functions of internal secretions. Restricts perspiration.

VIOLET

　Violet is a mixture of red and blue. Violet is a noble and precious color. Violet is called a neutral color. European violet, red-violet (purple) , red-violet = purple -> warm color, exciting color, advancing color. Japanese violet, blue-violet (violet) blue-violet = violet -> cool color, tranquilizing color, retreating color.

── Impressions of the color violet:

elegance, mysterious, sacred, authority, artistic, imagination, dignity, anxiety, solitude, mental instability, conceit

── Physiological and psychological effects of the color violet:

Decreases blood pressure and pulse. Hypnotic effect. Increases the power of imagination and creativity. Increases anxiety and stress. Curative effect, stimulates light-recovery enzymes in body and invigorates. Gives a feeling of solitude

BLACK, WHITE (ANCHORMA)

　Black is the color of absorbed light. White is the color of reflected light. Gray is mixed with black and white. Zero saturation colors are so-called achromatic colors such as white, gray and black.

── Impression of the achromatic color:

Black: defeat, devil, negative, inauspiciousness, fear, suppression, despair

White: win, innocence, clean, good, truth, alert, failure, loneliness

Gray: fecklessness, ambiguity, resignation, naught, anxiety, desperation

Color Samples

カラーサンプルについて

出品者から送付された情報をもとに、作品に掲載された印刷インクの色見本として、各クレジットの側にパントーン（PANTONE）ナンバーと色チップを掲載しました。出品者からの情報が不足している一部の作品については、小社で色判断をしました。本書は4色のプロセスカラーで印刷されていますので、実際の印刷インクとは多少異なる、参考程度の資料であることをあらかじめご了承ください。

With information provided by contributors and work submittors, we have included as color samples the PANTONE® Color reference numbers, and corresponding color chips of the printing inks used for each piece of artwork, as reference data next to each credit. For those few pieces for which this information was incomplete we have identified the inks ourselves. As this book has been printed in four colors, the colors may vary slightly from that of the actual printing inks.

また再現が難しい特殊加工については、下記記号で表記しました。
Special printing process is identified by the following symbol:

H .... 箔押し　Hot Stamping
B .... 空押し　Blank Stampin
E .... エンボス　Embossing
S .... シルク・スクリーン印刷　Screen Printing
T .... バーコ印刷　Thermography
U .... UVインク　Ultra Violet Ink
M .... マット・インク　Matt Ink
PE............ パール・インク　Pearl Ink
PH .... 畜光インク　Phosphorescent Ink
F .... 蛍光インク　Fluorescent Ink
PV............ ニス引き　Press Vanishing

PANTONE® のカラーリファレンスは著作権により保護されており、本書シリーズにおいてはPANTONE社の許諾を得て複製しております。読者の参考になるように、PANTONE（パントーン）社によって正確さを確認されたものではありません。カラー標準に関しては、現在発行中のPANTONEカラー・パブリケーションをご参照ください。

PANTONE® Color references are protected by copyright and are reproduced herein by permission of PANTONE, Inc. PANTONE-identified Color reproduction information has been provided for the guidance of the reader. The color have not been checked by PANTONE, Inc. for accuracy. Refer to current PANTONE Color Publications for the color standard.

PANTONE® は、PANTONE（パントーン）社の登録商標です。
PANTONE® is a registered trademark of PANTONE, Inc.

Editorial Note

レイアウト フォーマット ガイド

■ Color Samples （カラー・サンプル）

Screen combination and color density are included for works on pages 9 through 48.
P9-48の作品においては、作品に使用された2色の掛け合わせと濃度変化がわかる、
カラー・チャートを掲載しています。

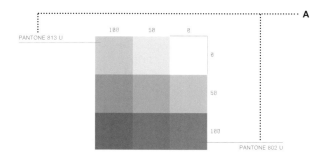

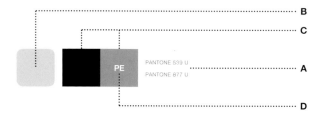

A	Printing inks are specified as PANTONE numbers. 印刷インクのPANTONEナンバー
B	Swatches of paperstock colors used in the work. 作品に使用された紙の色見本。
C	Swatches of ink colors used in the work. 作品に使用された印刷インクの色見本。
D	Abbreviations for special inks or finishing techniques used on the work (See pages 7 for key) 作品に使用された特殊加工、特殊インクの名称の略記号。 （記号についてはP7を参照。）

■ Credit Format （クレジット・フォーマット）

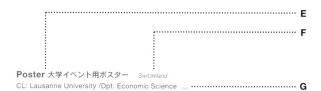

E	Work Form 作品内容
F	Country 出品者国名
G	CL: Client （クライアント） CD: Creative Director （クリエイティブ・ディレクター） AD: Art Director （アート・ディレクター） D: Designer （デザイナー） P: Photographer （撮影家・カメラマン） I: Illustrator （イラストレーター） CW: Copywriter （コピーライター） DF: Design Firm （デザイン事務所） SB: Submittor （出品者）

*At the request of the submittor, some works appear without credits.
*出品者の意向により、クレジット・データの一部を掲載していないものもあります。

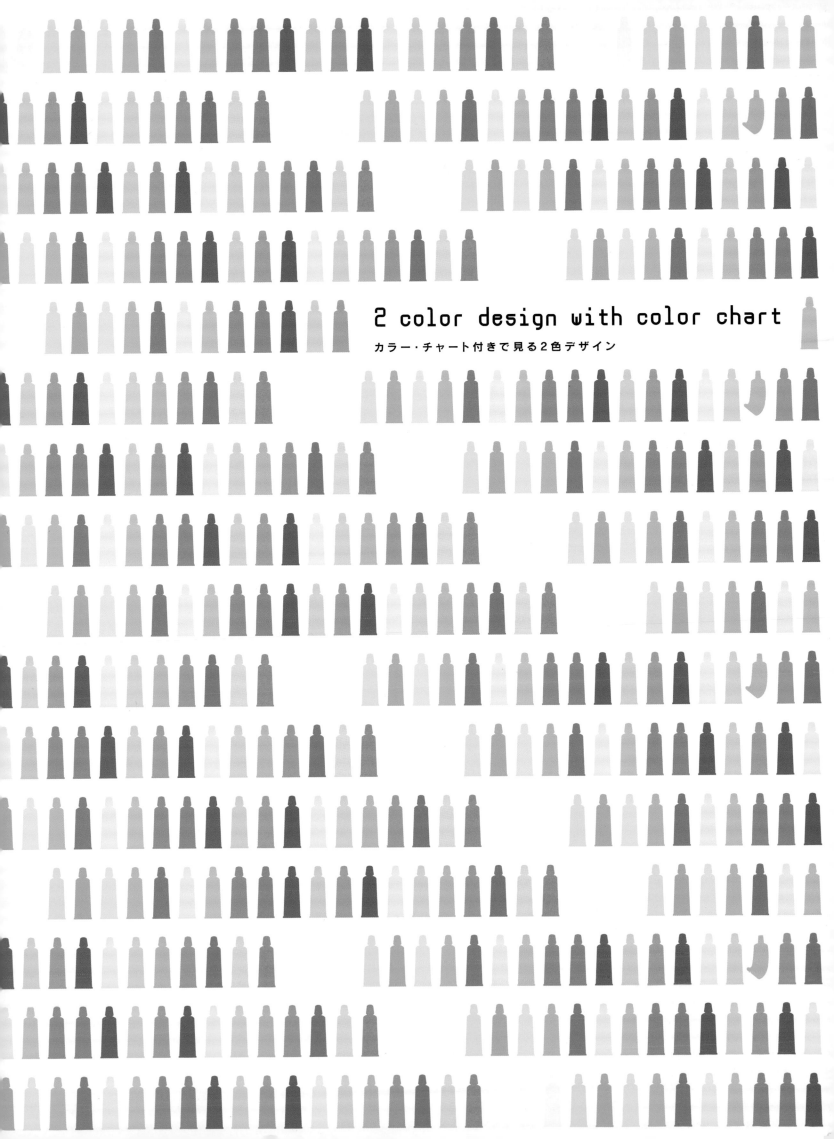

2 color design with color chart

カラー・チャート付きで見る2色デザイン

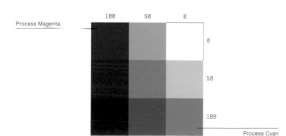

Poster 大学イベント用ポスター　*Switzerland*
CL: Lausanne University /Dpt. Economic Science　CD, AD, D: Cristiana Boli Freitas　I: Laurent Boli　DF: Bread and Butter

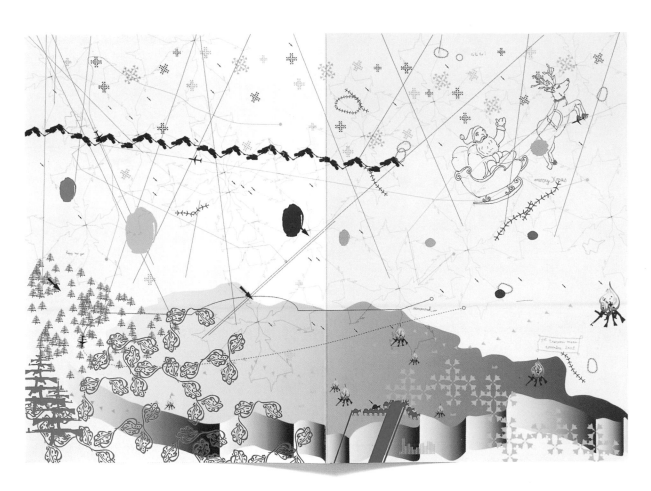

Event Pamphlet & Folder イベントパンフレット・フォルダー *Switzerland*
CL: Bread and Butter   CD, AD, D: Cristina Bolli Freitas   I: Laurent Bolli   DF: Bread and Butter

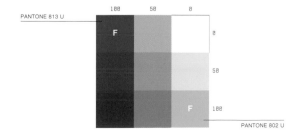

Publishing Guide Small Book 出版案内小型本　*The Netherlands*
CL: Malmberg Publisher　CD, AD, D: Petra Janssen, Edwin Vollebergh　CD, AD, D, DF: Studio Boot

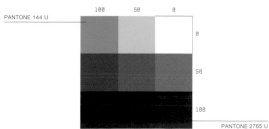

PANTONE 144 U

PANTONE 2765 U

Brochure 家具販売会社ブローシャー *USA*
CL: Urban Ease   D: Giorgio Davanzo   DF: Giorgio Davanzo Design

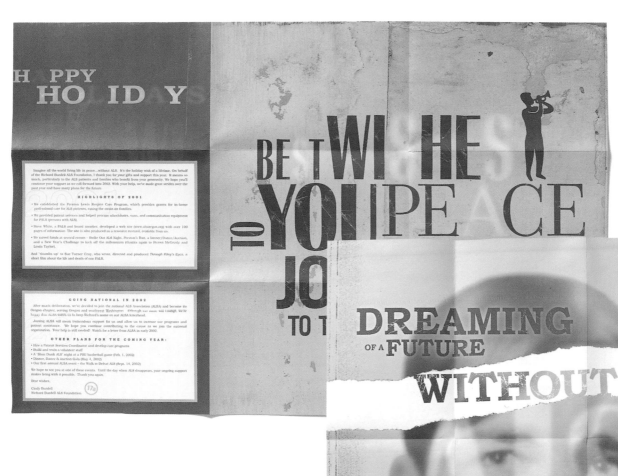

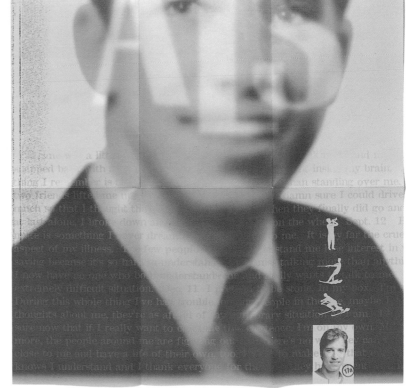

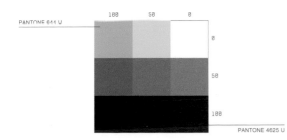

PANTONE 611 U

	100	50	0
0			
50			
100			

PANTONE 4625 U

Direct Mail & Poster 慈善団体DM・ポスター　*USA*
CL: ALS Association of Oregon & SW Washington　D: Karen Wippich　D, I: Jon Wippich　DF: Dotzero Design

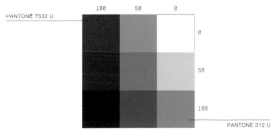

Poster & Stationery & Identity System ポスター・ステーショナリー一式　*Mexico*
CL: El Centro　DF: Blok Design

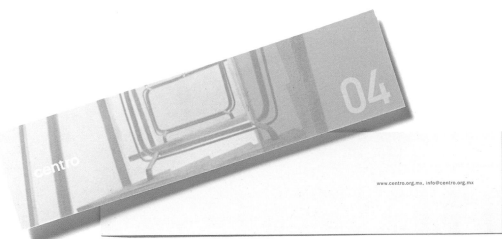

www.centro.org.mx, info@centro.org.mx

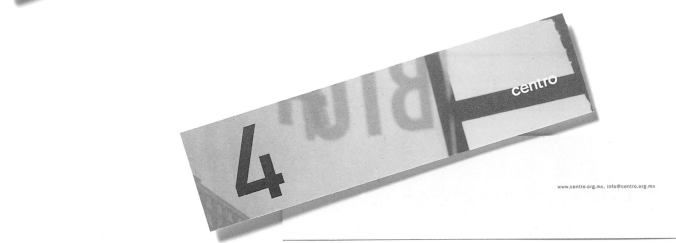

www.centro.org.mx, info@centro.org.mx

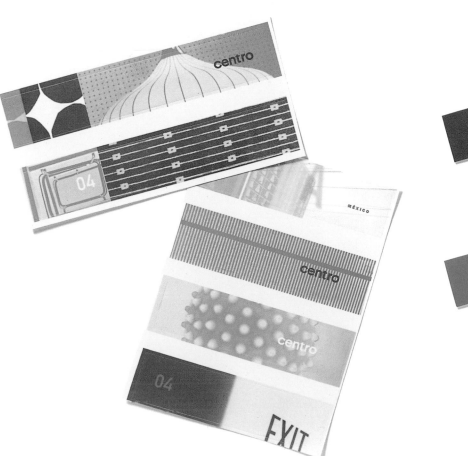

centro

145, lomas de chapultepec
11000 méxico df, tel. 5202 6017 | 4779
5520 4159 | 4152 | 8686 fax. 5520 8386
www.centro.org.mx, jbolado@centro.org.mx

JORGE BOLADO

centro

145, lomas de chapultepec
11000 méxico df, tel. 5202 6017 | 4779
5520 4159 | 4152 | 8686 fax. 5520 8386
www.centro.org.mx, jrosas@centro.org.mx

JORGE ROSAS

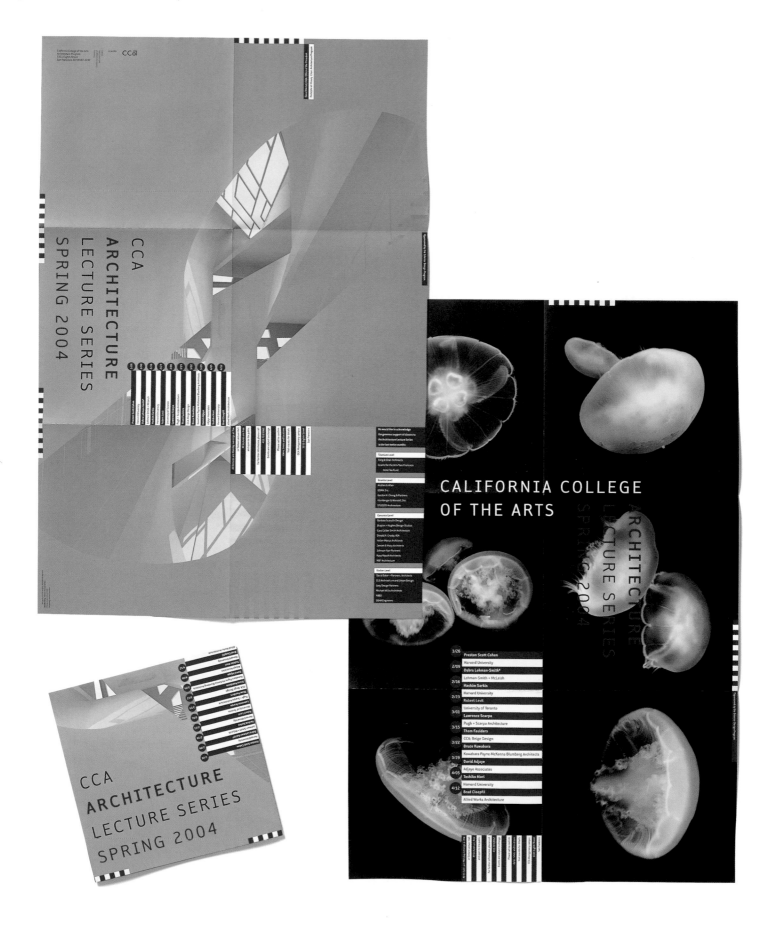

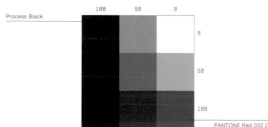

Poster 教育プログラムのポスター *USA*

PANTONE Red 032 C

CL: California College of Arts and Crafts Architecture Program   AD, D, P: Bob Aufuldish   DF: Aufuldish & Warinner

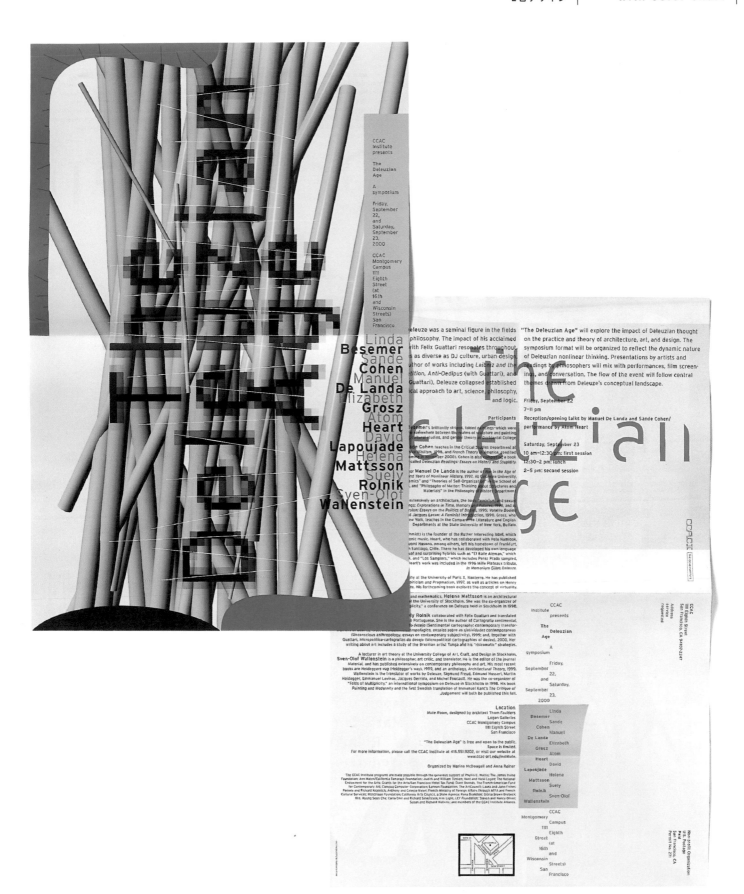

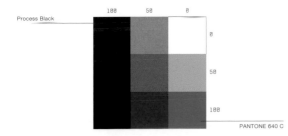

PANTONE 640 C

Flyer & Mailer 教育施設のフライヤー・DM　*USA*

CL: California College of Arts and Crafts Institute　AD, D: Bob Aufuldish　DF: Aufuldish & Warinner

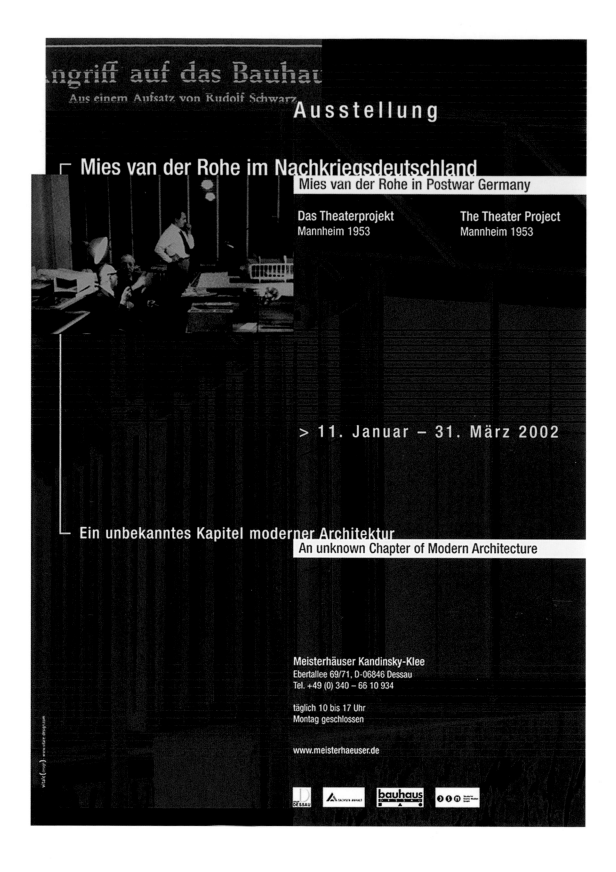

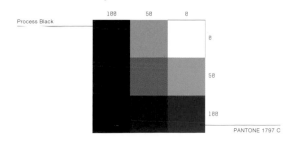

Process Black

100 50 0
0
50
100

PANTONE 1797 C

Poster, Invitation, Brochure, Catalog 展示会用ポスター・招待状・ブローシャー・カタログ *France*
CL: Bauhaus Dessau, City of Dessau AD, D: Steven Vitale D: Vincent Dietsch DF: Designhelden

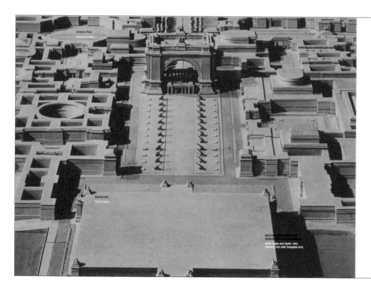

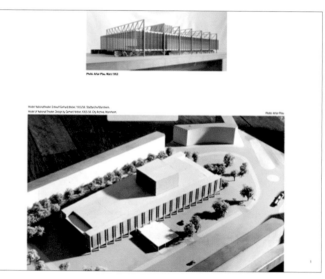

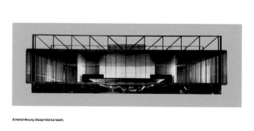

Process Black

100   50   0

PANTONE 1797 C

Brochure, Catalog 展示会用ブローシャー・カタログ   *France*
CL: Bauhaus Dessau, City of Dessau   AD, D: Steven Vitale   D: Vincent Dietsch   DF: Designhelden

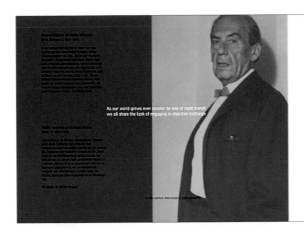

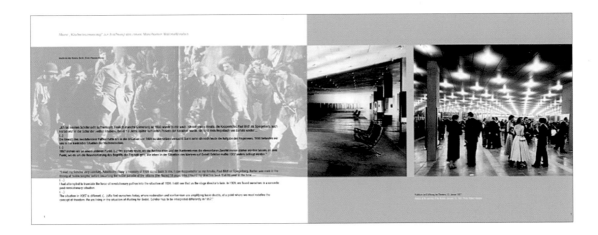

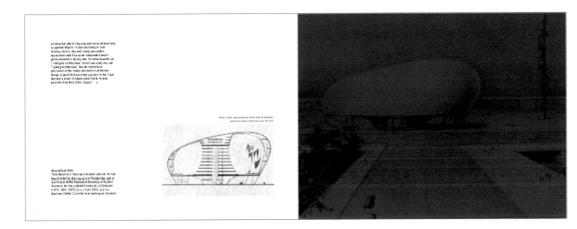

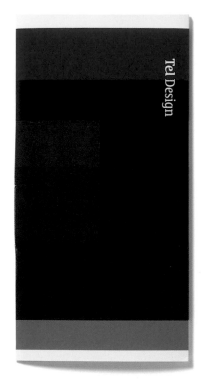

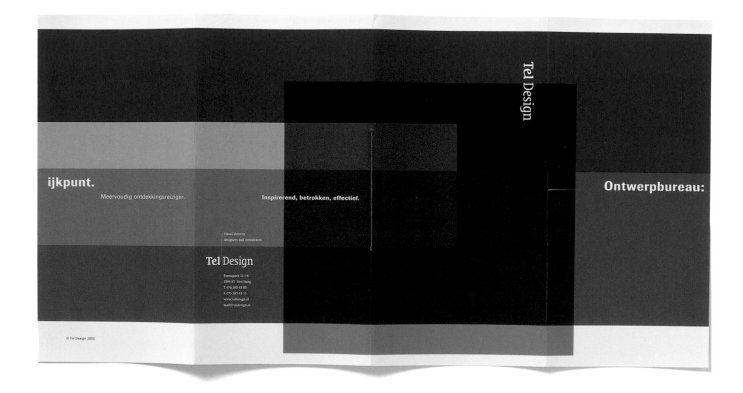

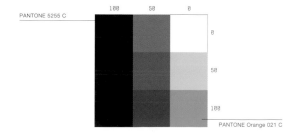

PANTONE 5255 C

PANTONE Orange 021 C

Brochure デザイン事務所 ブローシャー *The Netherlands*
CL: Tel Design   D: Jaco Emmen, Toon Tesser   DF: Tel Design

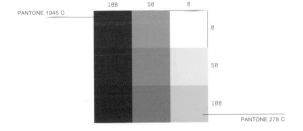

PANTONE 1945 C

PANTONE 278 C

Brochure ブローシャー　*The Netherlands*
CL: Tel Design　D: Jaco Emmen, Toon Tesser　DF: Tel Design

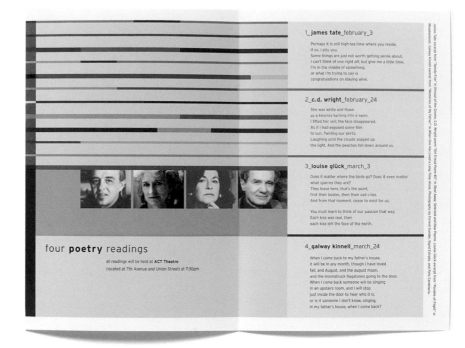

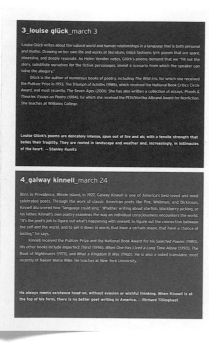

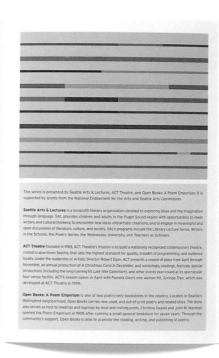

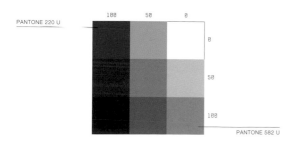

PANTONE 220 U

100   50   0

0

50

100

PANTONE 582 U

Brochure 芸術公共団体ブローシャー   *USA*
CL: Seattle Arts & Lectures   D: Karen Cheng   DF: Cheng Design

Brochure 教育施設ブローシャー *USA*
CL: California College of Arts and Crafts Office of Enrollment Services
AD, D, P: Bob Aufuldish DF: Aufuldish & Warinner

Brochure 学校案内 *USA*
CL: California College of Arts and Crafts AD, D, P: Bob Aufuldish
DF: Aufuldish & Warinner

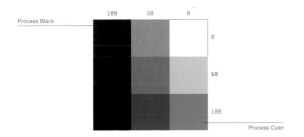

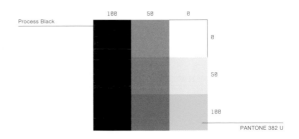

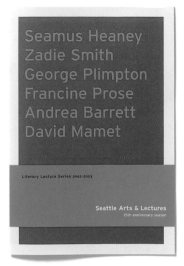

Seamus Heaney
Zadie Smith
George Plimpton
Francine Prose
Andrea Barrett
David Mamet

Literary Lecture Series 2002-2003

Seattle Arts & Lectures
15th anniversary season

2002-2003
Seattle Arts & Lectures

LITERARY LECTURE SERIES
Presented by the *Seattle Post-Intelligencer*

Seamus Heaney .... OCT 07
Zadie Smith .... NOV 12
George Plimpton .... JAN 21
Francine Prose .... FEB 18
Andrea Barrett .... MAR 11
David Mamet .... APR 01

BENEFIT PERFORMANCE

Ira Glass .... SEP 24

SPECIAL EVENTS

A New Generation of Mexican Poets .... OCT 29
An Evening with Tim O'Brien .... NOV 04

15th anniversary season

Seamus Heaney | Mon Oct 7
Benaroya Hall 7:30pm
In awarding Seamus Heaney the Nobel Prize for Literature in 1995, the Swedish Academy praised him "for works of lyrical beauty and ethical depth, which exalt everyday miracles and the living past." Born in 1939, in County Derry, the eldest of nine children, Heaney was raised on his parents' farm in Northern Ireland. His poetry is deeply marked by both his rural upbringing and his experience of political unrest. "He has often written of the poet as a kind of farmer," notes *The New York Times*, "as though Ireland's wet peat were a storehouse of images and memories." But violence is always intruding on this bucolic life, as he makes clear in his famous poem "Digging." "Between my finger and my thumb/The squat pen rests; snug as a gun."

Heaney's first poetry collections, *Death of a Naturalist* (1966) and *Door Into the Dark* (1969), earned him international acclaim. He has gone on to publish numerous collections of poetry, three works of criticism, and *The Cure at Troy* (1966), a version of Sophocles's *Philoctetes*. In 2000, Heaney published a new translation of *Beowulf*, turning the Anglo-Saxon epic into an international bestseller a thousand years after it was originally written. His most recent publications include *Opened Ground* (1998), *Diary of One Who Vanished* (2000), and *Electric Light* (2001).
Underwritten by Hoffman Construction Company of Washington.

"The most important Irish poet since Yeats."
–Robert Lowell

Zadie Smith | Tue Nov 12
Benaroya Hall 7:30pm
Like many precocious English majors, Zadie Smith began writing a novel during her senior year in college. But in her case, the novel was not only published, but went on to become an international bestseller, earning her comparisons to Salman Rushdie and Arundhati Roy. Epic in scale and intimate in approach, *White Teeth* (2000) navigates issues of race, gender, history, and culture in the eccentric lives of several Londoners. "Zadie Smith's debut novel is, like the London it portrays, a restless hybrid of voices, tones, and textures," wrote *The New York Times Book Review*. "Smith holds it all together with a raucous energy and confidence that couldn't be a fluke."

Born in 1976, the daughter of a Jamaican mother and British father, Smith grew up in North London. She graduated from Cambridge University in 1998. *White Teeth* won the Whitbread First Novel Award, the Guardian First Book Award, and the James Tait Black Memorial Prize for Fiction; it was also a finalist for the National Book Critics Circle Award and the Orange Prize. Currently, Smith is studying at Harvard University. Her second novel, *The Autograph Man*, is due out in October 2002.
Underwritten by The Central District Forum for Arts and Ideas

"Not since Mary Shelley composed *Frankenstein* at the age of 19 has a bookish young woman made such an extraordinary debut."
–The Baltimore Sun

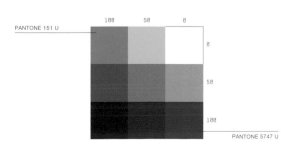

PANTONE 151 U

100   50   0

0

50

100

PANTONE 5747 U

Brochure 芸術公共団体ブローシャー   *USA*
CL: Seattle Arts & Lectures   D: Karen Cheng   DF: Cheng Design

"The seminar infused my teaching with great new energy."

2002-2003
teachers as scholars

Teachers are the largest and most important group of public intellectuals in our society, and if national efforts to raise standards are to succeed, teachers must be reinvigorated as academic thinkers and leaders. Teachers as Scholars is a professional development program that ignites and sustains the intellectual interests of K-12 teachers.

Content-based seminars led by university faculty are the centerpiece of the Teachers as Scholars model. Teachers as Scholars allows teachers to become students again and to immerse themselves in scholarly issues, regardless of the grade level they teach or their area of expertise. By participating in small seminars led by professors in the humanities, K-12 teachers are reconnected to the world of scholarship.

Teachers as Scholars is sponsored jointly by the Simpson Center for the Humanities at the University of Washington and Seattle Arts & Lectures, in association with events presented by the Burke Museum, ACT Theatre, the Henry Art Gallery, the Seattle Art Museum, the Seattle Repertory Theatre, and the Seattle Symphony.

The Simpson Center for the Humanities at the University of Washington is dedicated to fostering research and teaching in the humanities, and to stimulating exchange and debate on related intellectual, cultural, and educational issues. Its broader goal is to knit the academic and the civic communities through a shared fostering of education and culture. The Simpson Center sponsors a wide range of activities including outreach programs that encourage the participation of scholars in civic culture; and conversely, the participation of citizens in the life of the University.

Seattle Arts & Lectures (SAL) is a nonprofit literary arts organization devoted to exploring ideas and the imagination through language. SAL provides children and adults with opportunities to meet writers and cultural thinkers, to encounter new ideas and artistic creations, and to engage in meaningful conversations about literature, culture, and society. In addition to Teachers as Scholars, SAL's programs include a Literary Lecture Series, an annual poetry series, Writers in the Schools, and The Wednesday University.

Seminars in the Humanities for K-12 Teachers // Controversial Images: Telling the History of Modern Science / Modern Mexico in Art and Literature / American Song / Myth, Art, and Metamorphosis / Crossing Borders, Crossing Genres / Shostakovich and His Contemporaries: Early Soviet Art, Music, and Literature / Native Voices / How American is Asian American Literature? / Shakespeare's Tragedies: Text, Interpretation, Production / America: A Sentimental Adventure / The Great Migration / Latin American Artists and the Spanish Civil War

teachers as scholars
2002-2003

a program of the
Simpson Center for the Humanities
and **Seattle Arts & Lectures**

The Great Migration
Saturdays, Apr 26 and May 10, Seattle Art Museum and UW Simpson Center, 10am-2pm

In the early twentieth century, successive waves of out-migration from the rural South to the urban North remade black Americans into urbanites and remade the largest American centers into "chocolate cities," as they were called in popular culture. Collectively known as the "Great Migration," these flights formed an exodus from a land of slavery and persistent exploitation to a "land of hope." The Great Migration offered the hope of meaningful freedom and progress in the history of a people, and it presented "the Negro problem" as one for American society more widely. What set so many people flowing? How did family and social relations, gender ideals, southern planters, businessmen, police, northern black newspapers, and activists all play a part in the Great Migration? What did migrants find in the North, this "land of hope"? This seminar will explore these and other questions. Readings will address the roots, processes, and consequences of emigration from the South.

Associated Event:
Over the Line: The Art and Life of Jacob Lawrence, Seattle Art Museum, Feb-May 2003

Faculty:
Stephanie Camp

Latin American Artists and the Spanish Civil War
Saturdays, May 3 and 17, UW Simpson Center, 9am-1pm

The Spanish Civil War (1936-39) galvanized artists, intellectuals, poets, and working people throughout the world in defense of democracy in Spain. The war is still understood as the first armed confrontation between the forces of democracy and fascism. People came to the aid of the Spanish Republic in overwhelming numbers: 40,000 volunteers from over fifty countries joined the International Brigades to fight Franco's fascist troops. Artists and writers also turned their art to the defense of Spain, and Latin Americans were no exception. Two of the most outstanding poets of their generation, Pablo Neruda (Chile) and César Vallejo (Peru), wrote perhaps the most powerful books of poetry generated by that historic struggle. In addition, the works of the Mexican muralists from the same period—Diego Rivera, Orozco, Siqueiros—show a similar concern for the pressing social issues of the day. We will read Neruda's *Spain in the Heart* and Vallejo's *Spain, Take This Cup from Me* in the context of the poets' earlier works, as well as examine their works in the turn from avant-garde art to engagement that took place in the '30s. We will also consider the broader cultural and artistic themes of the twentieth century in Latin America.

Associated Event:
Viva la Musica!, Seattle Symphony, May 6-17

Faculty:
Anthony Geist

teachers as scholars faculty —→

"At the college level, we are often talking about the theory behind the practice and training of future K-12 teachers. This chance to discuss these complex theoretical, social, and educational issues with K-12 teachers provided me with new insights about the topics, from the linguistic situation in their classrooms to the ongoing educational needs and goals we face at every level."

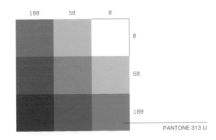

PANTONE 159 U

PANTONE 313 U

Brochure 芸術公共団体ブローシャー　*USA*
CL: Seattle Arts & Lectures, SImpson Center for the Humanities　D: Karen Cheng　DF: Cheng Design

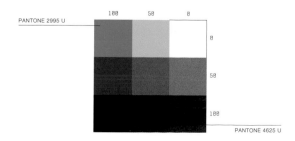

PANTONE 2995 U

PANTONE 4625 U

Cymposium Invitation & Program シンポジウム案内状・プログラム *The Netherlands*
CL: Homo Emancipatiebeleid   D: Kees Wagenaars   DF: CASE

Nature is one of the best places to look for patterns.

Nature repeats certain patterns all the time. These repeating patterns often exist because they save space or time. For example, honeycombs are made up of hexagons because they fit together without any spaces between each one. Patterns also exist for communication or defense. Fireflies blink patterns to each other to attract mates and a leopard's spots are a pattern that helps it to blend into its habitat.

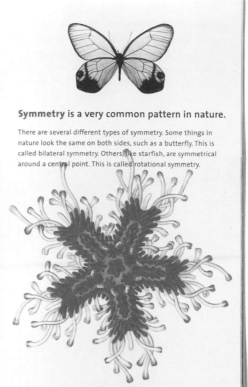

Symmetry is a very common pattern in nature.

There are several different types of symmetry. Some things in nature look the same on both sides, such as a butterfly. This is called bilateral symmetry. Others, like starfish, are symmetrical around a central point. This is called rotational symmetry.

*表紙は3色を使用。
Front Cover uses 3 colors.

While patterns are sometimes used to make safe and useful structures or objects, many times they are just for fun and decoration. In fact, you can find them just about anywhere you look, on wallpaper, fences, gates, clothes and bedspreads.

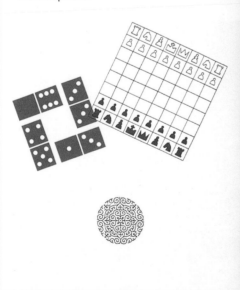

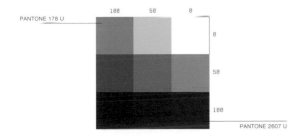

PANTONE 178 U

100   50   0

0

50

100

PANTONE 2607 U

Guide 児童博物館案内 *USA*
CL: Friends of Palo Alto Junior Museum and 200   D: Efrat Rafaeli   DF: Palo Alto Junior Museum - in House

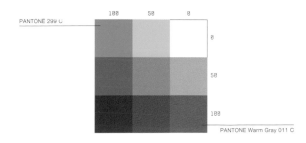

Poster 美術館ポスター *USA*
CL: Bellevue Art Museum   CD, AD: Kurt Wolken   D: Ryan Burlinson   DF: Wolken Communica

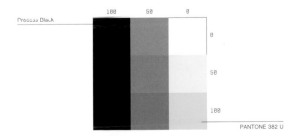

Brochure 美術館ブローシャー *USA*
CL: Bellevue Art Museum   CD, AD: Kurt Wolken   D: Ryan Burlinson   DF: Wolken Communica

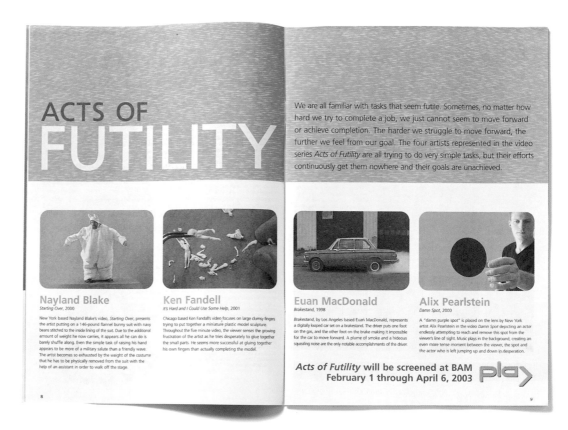

ACTS OF FUTILITY

We are all familiar with tasks that seem futile. Sometimes, no matter how hard we try to complete a job, we just cannot seem to move forward or achieve completion. The harder we struggle to move forward, the further we feel from our goal. The four artists represented in the video series *Acts of Futility* are all trying to do very simple tasks, but their efforts continuously get them nowhere and their goals are unachieved.

Nayland Blake
Starting Over, 2000

New York based Nayland Blake's video, *Starting Over*, presents the artist putting on a 146-pound flannel bunny suit with navy beans stitched to the inside lining of the suit. Due to the additional amount of weight he now carries, it appears all he can do is barely shuffle along. Even the simple task of raising his hand appears to be more of a military salute than a friendly wave. The artist becomes so exhausted by the weight of the costume that he has to be physically removed from the suit with the help of an assistant in order to walk off the stage.

Ken Fandell
It's Hard and I Could Use Some Help, 2001

Chicago based Ken Fandell's video focuses on large clumsy fingers trying to put together a miniature plastic model sculpture. Throughout the five minute video, the viewer senses the growing frustration of the artist as he tries desperately to glue together the small parts. He seems more successful at gluing together his own fingers than actually completing the model.

Euan MacDonald
Brakestand, 1998

Brakestand, by Los Angeles based Euan MacDonald, represents a digitally looped car set on a brakestand. The driver puts one foot on the gas, and the other foot on the brake making it impossible for the car to move forward. A plume of smoke and a hideous squealing noise are the only notable accomplishments of the driver.

Alix Pearlstein
Damn Spot, 2000

A "damn purple spot" is placed on the lens by New York artist Alix Pearlstein in the video *Damn Spot* depicting an actor endlessly attempting to reach and remove this spot from the viewer's line of sight. Music plays in the background, creating an even more tense moment between the viewer, the spot and the actor who is left jumping up and down in desperation.

Acts of Futility will be screened at BAM
February 1 through April 6, 2003

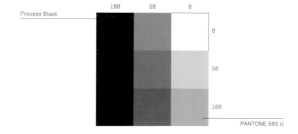

Magazine & Catalog 美術館カタログ雑誌 *USA*
CL: Bellevue Art Museum   CD, AD: Kurt Wolken   D: Johann Gomez   DF: Wolken Communica

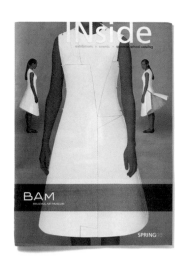

Publication Staff
Editor: Glen Miller
Design Firm: Walken Communica

Contributors: Sheryl Conkelton, Ginger Gregg
Duggan, Barbara Jirsa, Jennifer Knutson, Nancy
Looseen, Amy Rueffert, Alison Sievert, Miriam
Sternberg, Susan Todd, Karen Walker, Kirstie Warren

Spring 2003
INside is published four times per year:
Winter, Spring, Summer and Fall.
Bellevue Art Museum, 510 Bellevue Way NE,
Bellevue, WA 98004
Vol. 3 Issue 2

Cover Image: Hussein Chalayan, Remote Control Dress
Image courtesy of Fashion Group International

Sustained Museum support comes from the Allen
Foundation for the Arts, ArtsFund, Cultural Development
Authority of King County, Washington State Arts
Commission, Bellevue Arts Commission, Standing
Ovation and Bellevue Art Museum members and annual fund donors.

Location
Bellevue Art Museum
510 Bellevue Way NE
Bellevue, WA 98004

Bellevue Art Museum is located across
from Bellevue Square in downtown
Bellevue. Parking is free.

Exhibition Hours
Tuesday, Wednesday, Friday & Saturday,
10:00 a.m. – 5:00 p.m.
Thursday, 10:00 a.m. – 8:00 p.m.
Sunday, NOON – 5:00 p.m.

Admission
Adults $6
Seniors & Students $4
Children under age 6 are free.
Admission is free the third Thursday
and the last Saturday of each
month for all BAM visitors.

Telephone Numbers
Visitor Services   425.519.0770
School Information 425.519.0745
Membership   425.519.0751
Development   425.519.0749
Group Visits   425.519.0776
BAM Store   425.519.0772
Café 510   425.519.0772
Facility Usage   425.519.0744
Website   www.bellevueart.org

INside this Issue

Bellevue Art Museum inspires and enlightens an increasingly broad audience
through active encounters with modern and contemporary works of art, design,
architecture, and craft and an integrated approach to exhibiting and teaching.

1

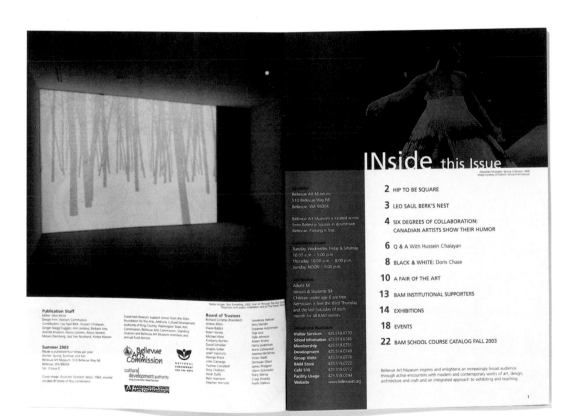

Publication Staff
Editor: Glen Miller
Design Firm: Walken Communica

Contributors: Leo Saul Berk, Hussein Chalayan,
Ginger Gregg Duggan, Ann Jacobus, Barbara Jirsa,
Jennifer Knutson, Nancy Looseen, Alison Sievert,
Miriam Sternberg, Jess Van Nostrand, Karen Warren

Summer 2003
INside is published four times per year:
Winter, Spring, Summer and Fall.
Bellevue Art Museum, 510 Bellevue Way NE,
Bellevue, WA 98004
Vol. 3 Issue 3

Cover Image: Eccentric Scientist, detail, 1964, enamel
on steel © Estate of Roy Lichtenstein

Sustained Museum support comes from the Allen
Foundation for the Arts, ArtsFund, Cultural Development
Authority of King County, Washington State Arts
Commission, Bellevue Arts Commission, Standing
Ovation and Bellevue Art Museum members and
annual fund donors.

Bellevue Art Museum
510 Bellevue Way NE
Bellevue, WA 98004

Bellevue Art Museum is located across
from Bellevue Square in downtown
Bellevue. Parking is free.

Tuesday, Wednesday, Friday & Saturday,
10:00 a.m. – 5:00 p.m.
Thursday, 10:00 a.m. – 8:00 p.m.
Sunday, NOON – 5:00 p.m.

Adults $6
Seniors & Students $4
Children under age 6 are free.
Admission is free the third Thursday and
the last Saturday of each
month for all BAM visitors.

Visitor Services   425.519.0770
School Information 425.519.0745
Membership   425.519.0751
Development   425.519.0749
Group Visits   425.519.0776
BAM Store   425.519.0772
Café 510   425.519.0772
Facility Usage   425.519.0744
Website   www.bellevueart.org

INside this Issue

Bellevue Art Museum inspires and enlightens an increasingly broad audience
through active encounters with modern and contemporary works of art, design,
architecture and craft and an integrated approach to exhibiting and teaching.

1

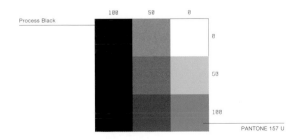

Process Black

PANTONE 157 U

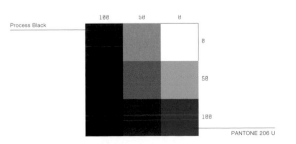

Process Black

PANTONE 206 U

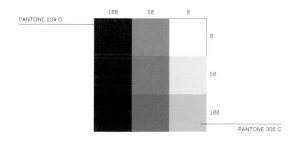

PANTONE 234 C

PANTONE 305 C

Leaflet 劇場プログラム用リーフレット　*The Netherlands*
CL: Gay Cinema　D: Kees Wagenaars　DF: CASE

9 EENMALIGE FILMDAGEN
ISM COC BREDA, TILBURG & EINDHOVEN
Gay Cinema 2003

Korte films van Bavo Defurne

Bavo Defurne maakt al jaren speelse films, vol mooie jongens in een wereld die het midden houdt tussen Pierre & Gilles en Jean Cocteau. De keuze voor charmante, onervaren spelers draagt bij tot zijn heel eigen wereld van zinnelijke erotiek en romantische onschuld. De filmtitels spreken voor zich: 'Atlantis', 'Kamyvour', 'Particularly now in spring', 'Matroos', 'Saint'. Ze geven een staalkaart van de grote thema's binnen de homo-erotica: de eerste grote liefde, het padvinderskamp, sportende schooljongens, matrozen en Sint Sebastiaan.
www.bavo.org.

Korte films van **Bavo Defurne**
Bavo Defurne • België 1990-1999, 56 min.

zo 09/03 Chassé Cinema Breda 16.15 uur
zo 09/03 Plaza Futura Eindhoven 17.15 uur
wo 12/03 Filmfoyer Tilburg 20.30 uur

The girl

Een jonge kunstenares raakt in de ban van een geheimzinnige nachtclubzangeres. Zx noemt haar 'the girl' en nodigt haar uit om samen de nacht door te brengen. Die ene nacht groeit onbedoeld uit tot een passionele affaire. Vanuit het duistere verleden van 'the girl' dreigt echter groot gevaar...

Het film noir-karakter van het verhaal naar de roman van Monique Wittig wordt onderstreept door de beelden van stille straatjes, oevers en bruggen van Parijs, zinderend van geheime hartstochten.

De film concentreert zich op de broeierige, nog ongerichte emoties. 'Madame Satâ' is een intens gnacteerde karakterstudie gevangen in krachtige beelden vol duistere schildering.
www.thegirl-themovie.com

The girl
Sande Zeiq • Frankrijk/VS 2000, 82 min.

zo 09/02 Plaza Futura Eindhoven 17.15 uur
zo 16/03 Chassé Cinema Breda 16.15 uur
wo 19/03 Filmfoyer Tilburg 20.30 uur

Madame Satâ

Naar het leven van de in 1976 overleden Braziliaanse straatvechter en dragqueen João Francisco dos Santos. Overdag werkend als ober en kok verdeelde hij in de jaren dertig zijn vrije tijd tussen gewelddadige criminele activiteiten en een bloeiende dragqueenverhouding. Dos Santos droomt van een beter en elegnter leven dan het prachtige kostuums en de glamour van de travestie.

Madame Satâ
Karim Ainouz • Brazilië 2001, 105 min.

zo 23/03 Plaza Futura Eindhoven 17.15 uur
zo 23/03 Chassé Cinema Breda 16.15 uur
wo 26/03 Filmfoyer Tilburg 20.30 uur

Sebastian - when everybody knows

De mannelijke tegenhanger van 'Fucking Åmål' en dus een mooie coming-out-film en de tweede met gevoel achterlaat. De 16-jarige Sebastian trekt veel op met een groepje vrienden en vriendinnen. Hij ging een tijdje verliefd is op zijn stoere klasgenoot Ulf. Thuis heeft Sebastian niets te klagen. Hij heeft een goede band met zijn ouders. Toch wil hij hen niet vertellen wat hem dwarszit. Als zijn ouders op een avond weg zijn nodigt hij Ulf uit. Samen maken ze er een enorme bende van, maar als Sebastian zijn klasgenoot op de mond kust is deze snel verdwenen...

Sebastian - *when everybody knows*
Svend Wam • Zweden/Noorwegen 1995, 86 min.

zo 30/03 Plaza Futura Eindhoven 17.15 uur
zo 30/03 Chassé Cinema Breda 16.15 uur
wo 02/04 Filmfoyer Tilburg 20.30 uur

9 EENMALIGE FILMDAGEN
ISM COC BREDA, TILBURG & EINDHOVEN
Gay Cinema 2003

Hush!

Naoya werkt in een dierenwinkel en gaat veel uit in het homocult. Maar hij heeft het gevoel dat er iets mist aan zijn relaxte, wat egocentrische leven. Katsuhiro houdt zijn homoseksualiteit joist verborgen voor zijn familie en omgeving, inclusief een collega die verliefd op hem is. Derde in het gezelschap is Asako, een vrouw met een psychiatrisch verleden en een kinderwens.

Regisseur Ryosuke ('Like grains of sand') brengt ze bij elkaar in een ingewikkelde driehoeksrelatie met zowel komische als tragische aspecten. 'Hush!' is een ontdekkingstocht naar andere invullingen van de hedendaagse familie, naar sociale omgangsvormen en verwachtingen.

Hush!
Hashiouchi Ryosuke • Japan 2001, 134 min.

zo 26/01 Chassé Cinema Breda 16.15 uur
zo 26/01 Plaza Futura Eindhoven 17.15 uur
wo 29/01 Filmfoyer Tilburg 20.30 uur

Kissing Jessica Stein

Jessica Stein is een emotionele en neurotische journaliste die aan het einde van haar latijn is. Haar broer heeft zich net verloofd, haar beste vriendin is zwanger, maar zelf heeft ze al jaren geen date meer gehad. Opeens valt haar oog op een contactadvertentie die echter wel in de 'vrouw zoekt-vrouw'-rubriek staat.

Ze ontmoet ze de hippe Helen Cooper en merkt ze tot haar verbazing dat het klikt. Een leuke avond met veel gelach en verhitte discussies eindigt in een zoen maar als Jessica verwart maar tegelijkertijd intrigeert.
www.2oosearchnight.com/kissingjessicastein

Kissing Jessica Stein
Charles Herman-Wurmfeld • VS 2002, 96 min.

zo 26/01 Chassé Cinema Breda 16.15 uur
zo 02/02 Plaza Futura Eindhoven 17.15 uur
wo 05/02 Filmfoyer Tilburg 20.30 uur

Presque rien

Mathieu brengt de zomer aan zee door. Hij helpt zijn zieke moeder en verdraagt zijn bemoeizuchtige oudere zus en vinnige zus. Op het strand ontdekt hij Cedric, een knappe, iets oudere jongen. Tussen de twee ontwikkelt zich al snel een romance, met dagen in de brandende zon en nachten vol gaheime ontmoetingen en passionele seks. Cedric heeft zijn school ingeruild voor een vaste maar eenvoudige baan en heeft zich in het verleden ook het vertrouwen van Mathieu's familieleden te winnen. Maar dan gaat er iets mis... Jaren later reist Mathieu terug naar de kust om uit te zoeken wat er gebeurd is.

Een glansrol is weggelegd voor Stephane Rideau ('Les roseaux sauvages', 'Sitcom', 'A toute vitesse') die perfect is als de agressieve maar kwetsbare Cedric.

Presque rien
Sébastien Lifahitz • Frankrijk 2000, 100 min.

zo 09/02 Chassé Cinema Breda 16.15 uur
zo 12/02 Filmfoyer Tilburg 20.30 uur
wo 16/03 Plaza Futura Eindhoven 17.15 uur

Lilies

Québec, 1952. Een bisschop wordt naar de gevangenis geroepen om de biecht af te nemen van de zieke Simon Doucet, die hem vertelt over zijn vroegere homoseksuele ervaringen. Als Simon enkele namen noemt schrikt de bisschop op: hij wordt herinnerd aan een driehoeksverhouding van veertig jaar geleden.

In zeer gestileerde vorm vertelt de film over zijn tragische liefdesgeschiedenis, over maatschappelijke hypocrisie, verlangen, verraad en berouw. 'Lilies' werd viervoudig bekroond met de nougste Canadese filmprijs.

Lilies
John Greyson • Canada 1996, 96 min.

zo 16/02 Chassé Cinema Breda 16.15 uur
zo 16/02 Plaza Futura Eindhoven 17.15 uur
wo 19/02 Filmfoyer Tilburg 20.30 uur

Lost and delirious

Perkins Girl's College is de gemiddelde meisjeskostschool, vol met gedragscodes, intriges en eenzaamheid. 'Mouse', een verliefd op een nieuw meisje, wordt snel geadopteerd door haar twee oudere kamergenotes: de scherpzinnige Paulie en de aantrekkelijke Victoria. Ze ontdekt al gauw dat Paulie en Victoria niet vaak apart slapen. De drie worden gezworen vriendinnen, maar de verhoudingen komen onder druk te staan wanneer Victoria begint met een jongen.

Het thema van Léa Pool's eerste engelstalige film is weliswaar uitgesproken lesbisch, maar verkolt evenzeer de passies en ondpoorheden van anders tienertijd.

Lost and delirious
Léa Pool • Canada 2001, 100 min.

zo 23/02 Chassé Cinema Breda 16.15 uur
zo 23/02 Plaza Futura Eindhoven 17.15 uur
wo 26/02 Filmfoyer Tilburg 20.30 uur

Lid worden van het COC? JA!

Zoenende jongens, twee lesbische vrouwen die samen kinderen opvoeden, een openlijk homoseksuele leerkracht: homoseksualiteit is in onze maatschappij steeds zichtbaarder. Maar vanzelfsprekend is het nog niet. De familiewetgeving houdt slechts ten dele rekening met de situatie waarin twee vrouwen of mannen een kind opvoeden. En lang niet iedere homo- of lesbienne kan op het werk openlijk praten over zijn of haar liefdesleven.

Daarom bestaat het COC, een federatie van 27 verenigingen in Nederland, waaronder een in Breda, Tilburg en Eindhoven. Word lid en steun deze belangenvereniging: de contributie bedraagt € 40 per jaar. Stuur deze bon op naar:
COC Nederland, Antwoordnummer 2966, 1000 RA Amsterdam of meld je aan via www.coc.nl.

Met dank aan de Vereniging van Gelukkige Filmlevelers en het COC. Programmering: Jeffry Bakshan, Chassé Cinema / Breda; Eric van Gorcken / Victoria: Kees Wagenaars, Breda

Naam		M/V
Adres		
Postcode	Plaats	
Geboortedatum	Telefoon	
e-mailadres		
Rekeningnummer	Handtekening	
Datum	Handtekening	

Alle voorstellingen in Chassé Cinema, Claudius Prinsenlaan 8, Breda 076-5303131 www.chasse.nl • Filmfoyer Tilburg, Schouwburgring, Tilburg 013-5490302 www.filmfoyer.nl • Plaza Futura Eindhoven, Leenderweg 65, Eindhoven 040-2946648 www.plazafutura.nl

Kortingsprijzen gelden op vertoon van Chassé Pas, Filmfoyer Pas, Plaza Pas of COC-lidmaatschapskaart.

9 EENMALIGE FILMDAGEN
ISM COC BREDA, TILBURG & EINDHOVEN
Gay Cinema 2003

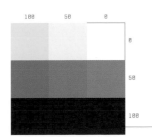

PANTONE 109 C

PANTONE 242 C

Leaflet 劇場プログラム用リーフレット   *The Netherlands*
CL: Gay Cinema   D: Kees Wagenaars   DF: CASE

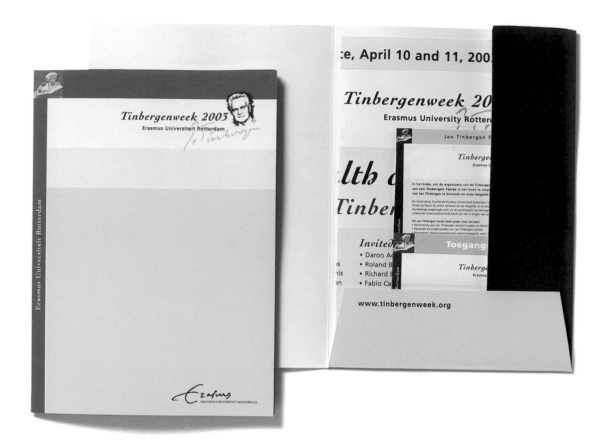

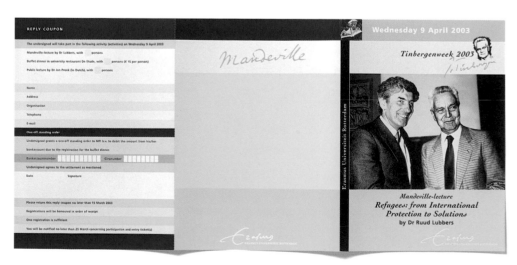

International Conference, April 10 and 11, 2003

Tinbergenweek 2003
Erasmus University Rotterdam

On the Wealth of Nations
Extending the Tinbergen heritage

Erasmus University Rotterdam

Feature of the conference

On April 12, 2003, it is a 100 years ago that Jan Tinbergen, first Nobel Laureate in Economics, was born. Erasmus University Rotterdam celebrates this event with a conference, featuring the connection between economic science and policy.
There are three major themes:

- **The dynamics of business cycles and the relevance of economic policy**
- **Policy effectiveness in economic growth, education, income distribution, and the labour market**
- **Globalisation and poverty**

Invited speakers include

- Daron Acemoglu (MIT)
- Roland Benabou (Princeton University)
- Richard Blundell (University College London)
- Fabio Canova (University of Pompeu Fabra)
- James Heckman, Nobel laureate, (University of Chicago)
- Dale Jorgensen (Harvard University)
- Adrian Pagan (Oxford University and University of New South Wales)
- Danny Quah (London School of Economics)
- Robert Shimer (Princeton University)
- Chris Sims (Princeton University)
- T.N. Srinivasan (Yale University)
- James Stock (Harvard University)

Call for papers

The programme will consist of invited and contributed papers on the three themes of the conference.
For further information on submission of papers visit the web site: www.tinbergenweek.org
Submissions must be received by January 10, 2003.

Scientific Programme Committee

H.K. van Dijk, chairman, G. van den Berg, A.L. Bovenberg, D.J.C. van Dijk, J. Francois, P.H.B.F. Franses, J.W. Gunning, B. Hoekman, C.N. Teulings, A. Venables

www.tinbergenweek.org

ERASMUS UNIVERSITEIT R

Jan Tinbergen Fonds

Tinbergenweek 2003
Erasmus Universiteit Rotterdam

Toegangskaart

Tinbergenweek 2003
Erasmus Universiteit Rotterdam

DRINKS & DINNER
Woensdag 9 april, aanvang 17.30 uur
Drinks Faculty Club
Dinner KR&Zv De Maas

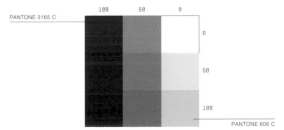

PANTONE 3165 C

100   50   0

0

50

100

PANTONE 606 C

Folder with Poster, Leaflet and Admission Ticket 大学広報素材一式（フォルダー・ポスター等） *The Netherlands*
CL: Erasmus University Rotterdam   CD: Arno Bauman   D: Jan Pinto   DF: Studio Bauman

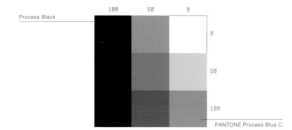

Brochure 施設 ブローシャー   *The Netherlands*
CL: Boumanhuis   CD, P: Arno Bauman   D: Emmy van Harskamp   P: Pepijn Lutgerink, Angelo Goedemond, Gemeente Archief Rotterdam, Enriques Tonelero
DF: Studio Bauman

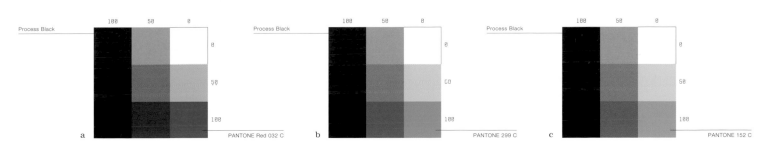

Brochure 学校案内 *USA*
CL: School of Occupational & Environmental Hygiene   AD: Michael Pacey   D: Robert Pacey   DF: Pacey + Pacey

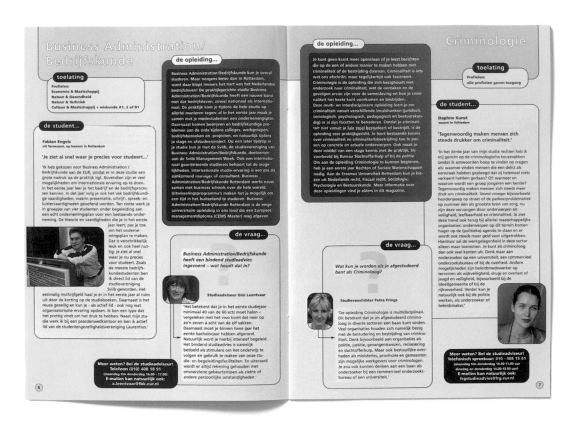

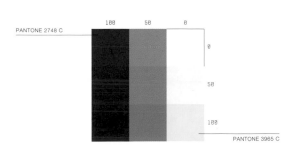

PANTONE 2748 C

PANTONE 3965 C

Brochure 学校案内 *The Netherlands*
CL: Erasmus University Rotterdam CD, P: Arno Bauman D: Jan Pinto
P: Claudine Grin, Ronald van den Heerik, Maarten Laupman, Levine Willemse DF: Studio Bauman

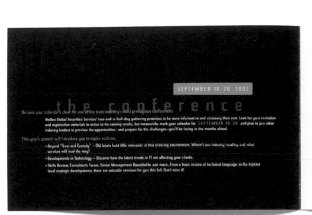

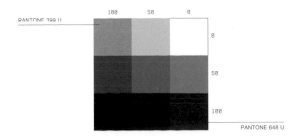

100 50 0

PANTONE 399 U

0

50

100

PANTONE 648 U

Event Identity & Invitation イベント招待状 *USA*
CL: Mellon   CD, AD: Natalie Pangaro, Shannon Beer   D: David Salafia   P: Sandra Baker   DF: Pangaro Beer Design

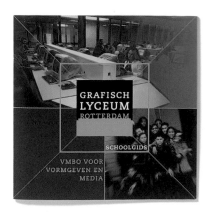

*表紙は4色を使用。
Front Cover uses 4 colors.

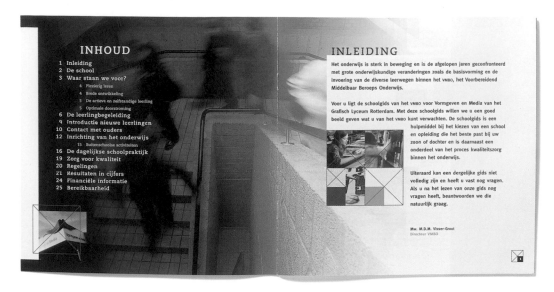

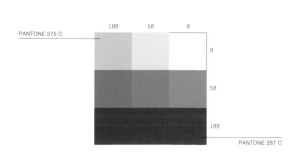

PANTONE 375 C

100   50   0

0

50

100

PANTONE 287 C

Brochure 学校案内 *The Netherlands*

CL: Grafisch Lyseum   CD, P, I: Arno Bauman   D, I: Inge van der Ploeg   DF: Studio Bauman

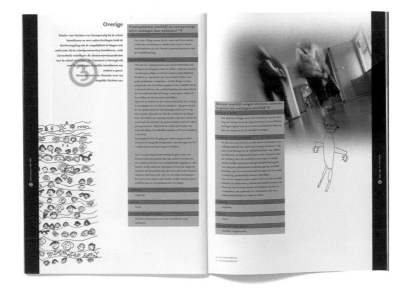

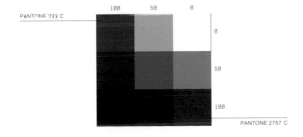

PANTONE ??? C

PANTONE 2757 C

Brochure 教育委員会 ブローシャー   *The Netherlands*
CL: Landelijke Klachtencommissie   CD, P: Arno Bauman   D: Emmy van Harskamp   DF: Studio Bauman

PANTONE 8560 U

100　　50　　0

PE

0

50

100

PANTONE 294 U

Stationery アパレル会社ステーショナリー　*Switzerland*

CL: Rodrigo Soares Studio　CD, AD, D: Cristina Bolli Freitas　I: Laurent Bolli　DF: Bread and Butter

a

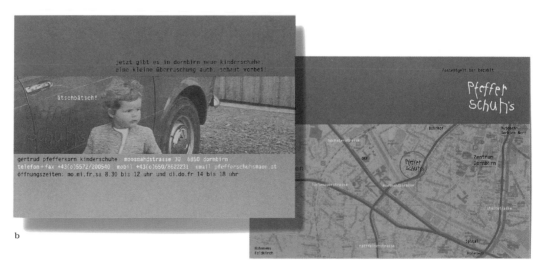

b

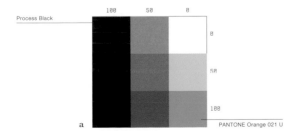

Process Black

100   50   0

0

50

100

a   PANTONE Orange 021 U

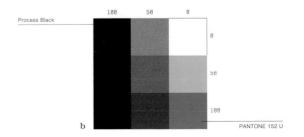

Process Black

100   50   0

0

50

100

b   PANTONE 152 U

MIscellaneous Stationery 大学のステーショナリー一式　*USA*
CL: California College of Arts and Crafts　AD, D: Bob Aufuldish　DF: Aufuldish & Warinner

Postcard 子供靴専門販売店PR用ポストカード　*Austria*
CL: Pfefferkorn　CD: Sigi Ramoser　D: Marcel Schrattner　DF: Sagenvier Designkommunikation

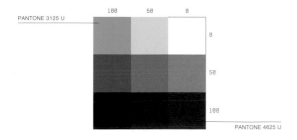

PANTONE 3125 U

PANTONE 4625 U

Poster & Program & Leaflet & Flyer　劇団PR用ポスター・プログラム・リーフレット・フライヤー　*The Netherlands*

CL: Teater '77　D: Kees Wagenaars　DF: CASE

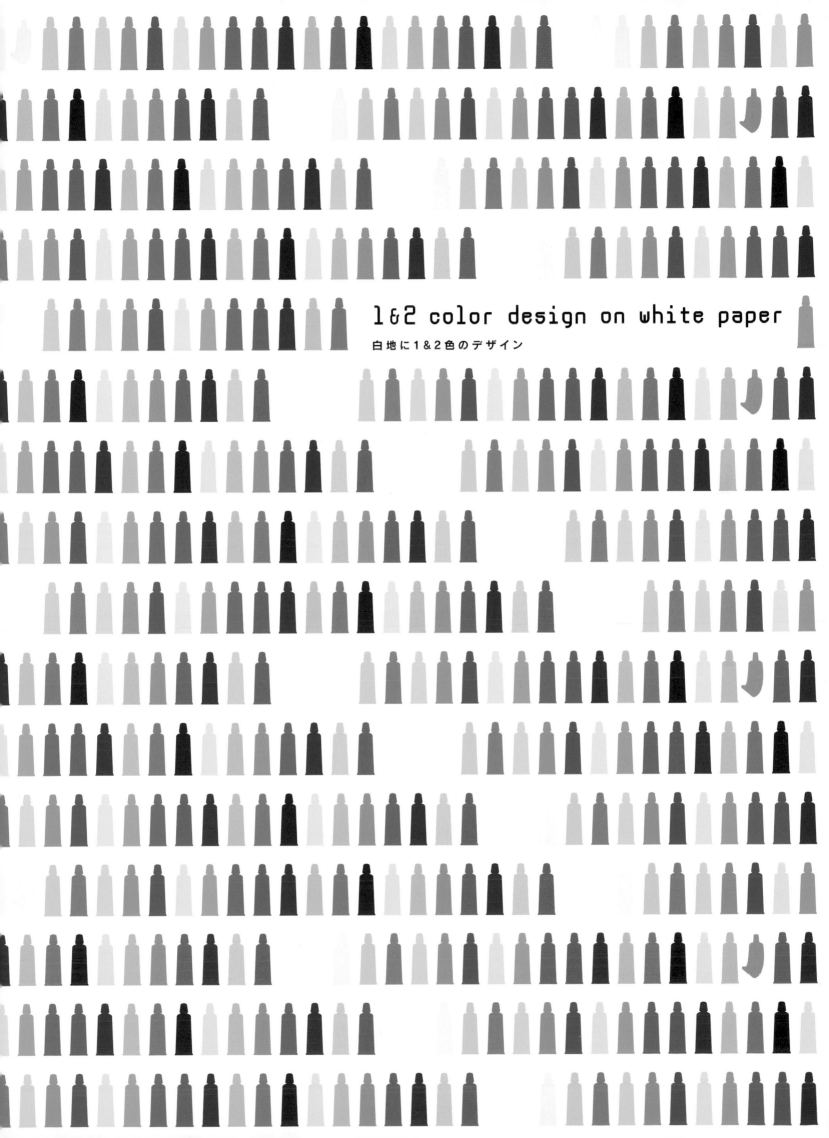

1&2 color design on white paper

白地に1&2色のデザイン

PE — PANTONE 289 U / PANTONE 877 U

Poster スケートボード大会用ポスター *USA*
CL: Lakai Limited Footwear   AD, D, P: Andy Mueller   DF: The Art Dump/ Ohio Girl Design

白地に1＆2色の
デザイン | 1&2 color design
on white paper | 051

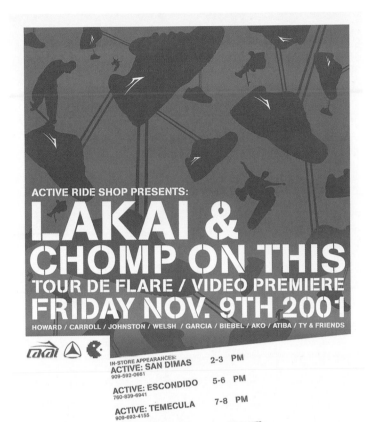

PANTONE 160 U

PANTONE 152 U

Poster スケートボード大会用ポスター　*USA*
CL: Lakai Limited Footwear　AD, D, I: Andy Mueller　DF: The Art Dump/ Ohio Girl Design

Process Black

PANTONE 637 U

Poster スケートボード大会用ポスター　*USA*
CL: Lakai Limited Footwear　AD, D, I: Andy Mueller　DF: The Art Dump/ Ohio Girl Design

a

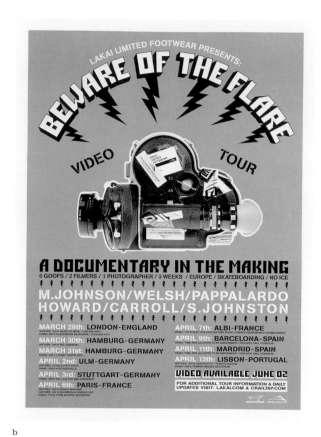

b

c

		Process Black
a		PANTONE 368 U

		Process Black
b	PE	PANTONE 877 U

		Process Black
c		PANTONE 151

Poster スケートボード大会用ポスター *USA* *a, b
CL: Lakai Limited Footwear   AD, D, P: Andy Mueller   DF: The Art Dump/ Ohio Girl Design

Poster スケートボード大会用ポスター *USA* *c
CL: Girl Skateboards   CD, AD, D, P: Andy Mueller   DF: The Art Dump/ Ohio Girl Design

白地に1＆2色の
デザイン | **1&2 color design
on white paper** | 053

a

b

c

d

a | Process Black / PANTONE 382 U

b | Process Black / PANTONE 298 U

c | PANTONE 260 / PANTONE 1375

d | PANTONE 350 / PANTONE 290

Poster スケートボード大会用ポスター　*USA*　*a, b
CL: Lakai Limited Footwear　AD, D: Andy Mueller　DF: The Art Dump/ Ohio Girl Design

Poster アート展覧会用ポスター　*USA*　*c, d
CL: Walled City Gallery　AD, D, I: Andy Mueller　DF: Ohio Girl Design with The Girl Dump

a

b

a — Process Black / PANTONE 137 C

b — Process Black / PANTONE 165 C

CD Cover CDジャケット *USA*

CL: Shiner/ Desoto Records   CD, AD, D, P: Andy Mueller   DF: Ohio Girl Design

白地に1＆2色の
デザイン | 1&2 color design
on white paper | 055

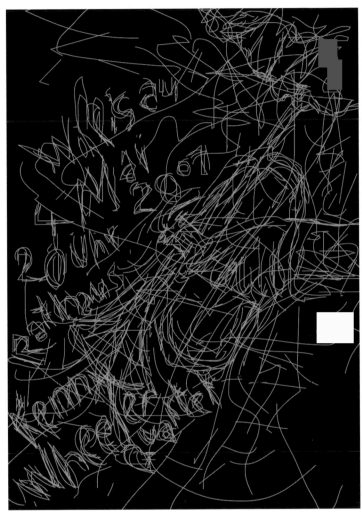

PANTONE Red 032
PANTONE Process Blue

Process Black
Process Cyan

Concert Poster 音楽コンサートポスター *Switzerland*
CL: Jazz in Willisau   CD, AD, D: Niklaus Troxler   DF: Niklaus Troxler Design

Concert Poster 音楽コンサートポスター *Switzerland*
CL: Jazz in Willisau   CD, AD, D: Niklaus Troxler   DF: Niklaus Troxler Design

Process Black
PANTONE 802 U

Poster ポスター *Germany*
CL: 100 Best Posters e.v.   DF: Cyan

PANTONE 806 U
PANTONE 873 U

Poster ポスター *Germany*
CL: 100 Best Posters e.v.   DF: Cyan

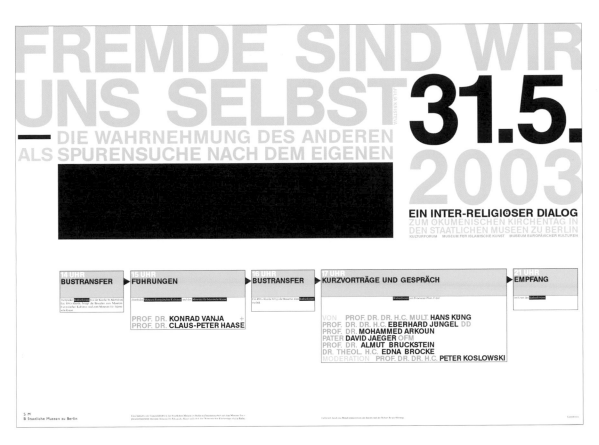

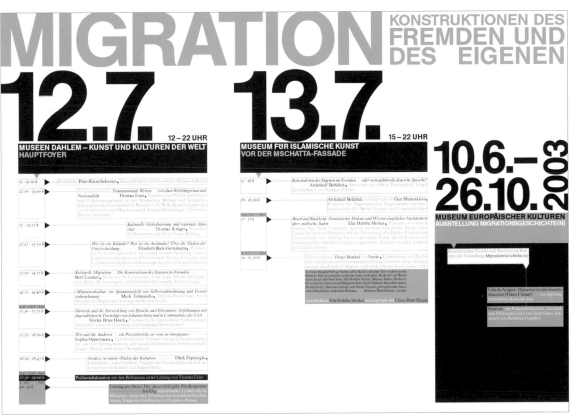

Process Black
PANTONE 802

Process Black
PANTONE 810

Poster 美術館ポスター　*Germany*
CL: Staatliche Museen zu Berlin　DF: Cyan

PANTONE 497 U

PANTONE 305 U

Process Black

PANTONE 1585 U

Poster 劇団PR用ポスター *The Netherlands*
CL: KROV D: Kees Wagenaars DF: CASE

Poster 劇団PR用ポスター *The Netherlands*
CL: Teater '77 D: Kees Wagenaars DF: CASE

PANTONE 136 U

PANTONE 2765 U

PANTONE 225 C

PANTONE 305 C

PANTONE 307 U

PANTONE 4625 U

Poster 劇団PR用ポスター *The Netherlands*
CL: BOXtheater D: Kees Wagenaars P: Paula Verheyen DF: CASE

Invitation Postcard 劇団案内状 *The Netherlands*
CL: KROV D: Kees Wagenaars DF: CASE

Invitation Postcard 劇団案内状 *The Netherlands*
CL: BOXtheater D: Kees Wagenaars DF: CASE

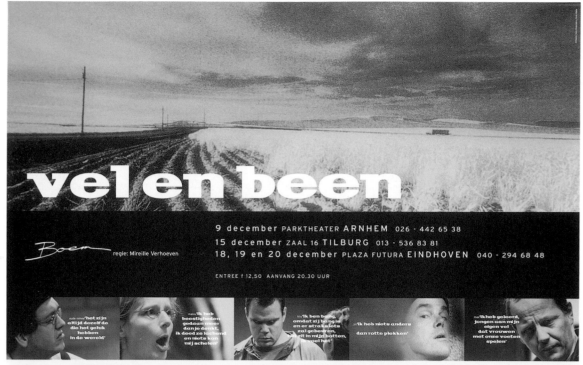

| PANTONE 235 U | | PANTONE 110 U |
| PANTONE 605 U | | PANTONE 1817 U |

Poster 劇団PR用ポスター　*The Netherlands*
CL: Boems　D: Kees Wagenaars　P: Rob Stork　DF: CASE

Poster 劇団PR用ポスター　*The Netherlands*
CL: KROV　D: Kees Wagenaars　DF: CASE

白地に1&2色の
デザイン | 1&2 color design
on white paper | 061

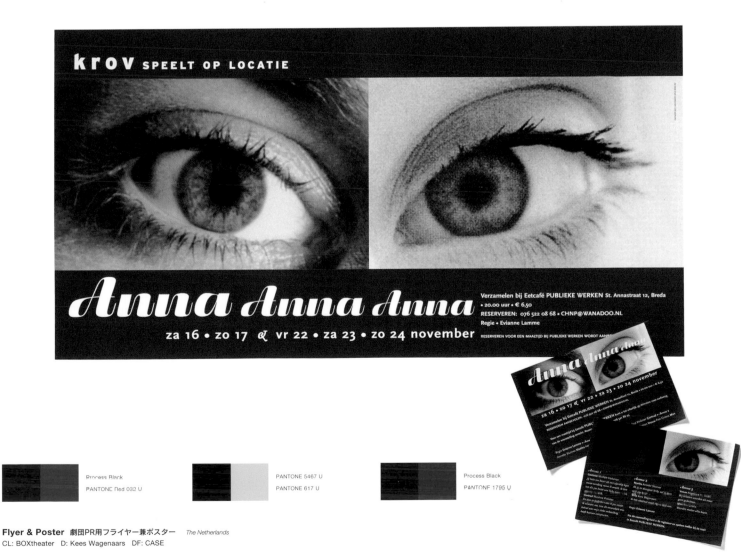

Flyer & Poster 劇団PR用フライヤー兼ポスター　*The Netherlands*
CL: BOXtheater　D: Kees Wagenaars　DF: CASE

Poster 劇団PR用ポスター　*The Netherlands*
CL: BOXtheater　D: Kees Wagenaars　DF: CASE

Flyer & Poster 劇団PR用フライヤー兼ポスター　*The Netherlands*
CL: KROV　D: Kees Wagenaars　DF: CASE

PE | DIC 621 (≈PANTONE 877)
DIC 2020 (≈PANTONE 1205)

Message Poster カフェ メッセージポスター   *Japan*
CL: Pousse Cafe Inc.   ブース・カフェ   AD, D: Kenji Umetani   梅谷健司

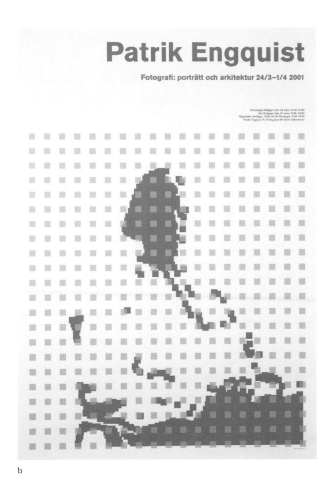

Patrik Engquist

Fotografi: porträtt och arkitektur 24/3–1/4 2001

b

a

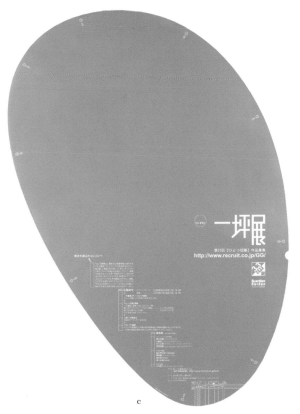

http://www.recruit.co.jp/GG/

c

Poster, Catalog & Invitation デザイン・工芸学校のポスター・カタログ他　*Sweden*　*a
CL: Swedish Society of Craft and Design　CD, AD, D: Markus Mostrom　DF: Markus Mostrom Design

Poster 写真家作品展示会ポスター　*Sweden*　*b
CL: Patrik Envist　CD, AD, D: Markus Mostrom　DF: Markus Mostrom Design

Poster 「一坪展」ポスター　*Japan*　*c
CL: Recruit Co., Ltd.　（株）リクルート　AD, D: Jun Kosaka　小阪淳

Process Black
PANTONE Warm Grey 9 U

a

PE　PE

PANTONE Black
PANTONE Warm Grey 9 U

b

PE　DIC 621 C (≒PANTONE 877 C)

c

F PANTONE 805 U 2X

Poster イベント用ポスター　*Switzerland*

CL: Tearoom Edition 2001 and 2002　CD, AD, D: Cristiana Boli Freitas　I: Laurent Boli　DF: Bread and Butter

白地に1＆2色の
デザイン | **1&2 color design
on white paper** | 065

Process Reflex Blue C

PANTONE 354 C

PANTONE Rubine Red C

PANTONE 354 C

Poster ポスター *Switzerland*
CL: Luzerner Apotheker Verein   AD, D, P: Niklaus Troxler   DF: Niklaus Troxler Design

Concert Poster ジャズコンサート ポスター *Switzerland*
CL: Jazz in Willisau   AD, D, P: Niklaus Troxler   DF: Niklaus Troxler Design

白地に1&2色の
デザイン | 1&2 color design
on white paper | 067

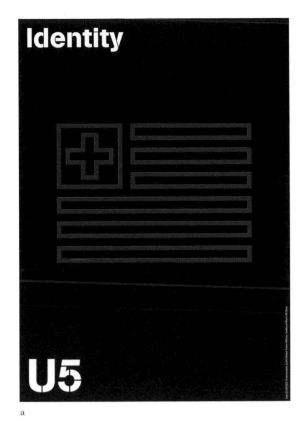

a

b

c

d

a

Process Black
PANTONE Rhodamine Red

b

Process Black
PANTONE 804

Process Black
c

PANTONE 2935
PANTONE 877

d

Process Black
PANTONE Red 032

Theatre Poster 演劇 ポスター *Switzerland* *a, b
CL: UNESCO/ EXPO 02   AD, D, P: Niklaus Troxler   DF: Niklaus Troxler Design

Concert Poster ジャズコンサート ポスター *Switzerland* *c, d
CL: Jazz in Willisau   AD, D, P: Niklaus Troxler   DF: Niklaus Troxler Design

cie. toula limnaios

better days
[ua]

4. – 7.
11. – 14.
18. – 21. 12. 2003
jeweils 20:30 h in der halle eberswalder str 10–11 10437 berlin
kartentelefon 440 44 292
eintritt 10 euro ermäßigt 8 euro

Process Black
PANTONE Warm Red U

Poster ポスター *Germany*
CL: Cie.ToulaLimnaios   DF: Cyan

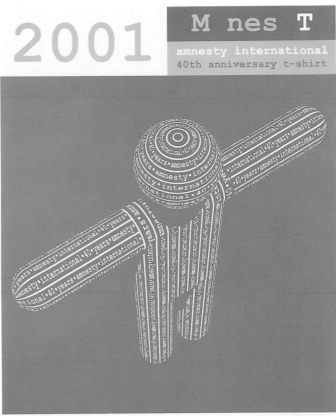

F PE PANTONE 812 U
PANTONE 8002 U

F PE PANTONE 802 C
PANTONE 877 C

Poster 眼鏡製造会社イメージポスター　　*Hong Kong*
CL: Kong Chung Hing Industrial Limited　AD, D: Joseph Leung　DF: Motakding Design

Poster アパレル会社ポスター　　*The Netherlands*
CL: Pepe Jeans London　AD, D: Boy Bastiaens　I: Albert Kiefer　DF: StormHand

Process Black
PANTONE 284 U

Process Black
PANTONE 142 U

Process Black
PANTONE 382 U

Process Black
PANTONE 237 U

Poster ギャラリーポスター *Germany*
CL: Singuhr D: M DF: Cyan

PANTONE 323 C
PANTONE 106 C

PANTONE 483 C
PANTONE 584 C

PANTONE 262 C
PANTONE 379 C

PANTONE 581 C
PANTONE 636 C

Poster 公共教育機関ポスター　*USA*
CL: Simpson Center for Humanities at the University of Washington　D: Karen Cheng　DF: Cheng Design

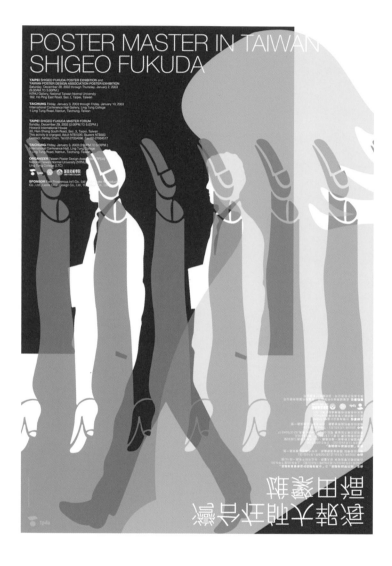

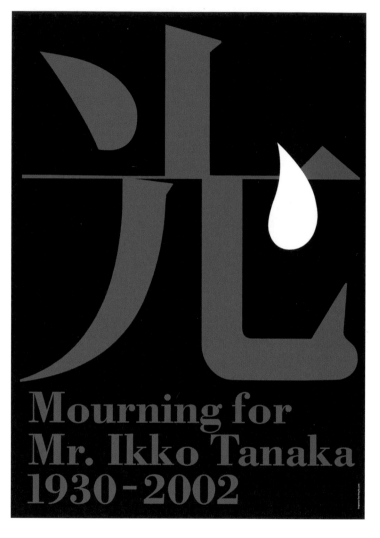

PANTONE Yellow C

PANTONE 185 C

Process Black

PANTONE 425 C

Poster 台湾デザイン協会展示会用ポスター　*Taiwan*
CL: Taiwan Poster Design Association　CD, AD, D: Leslie Chan Wing Kei　DF: Leslie
Chan Design Co. Ltd.

Poster 展示会用ポスター　*Taiwan*
CL: Leslie Chan Design Co. Ltd.　CD, AD, D: Leslie Chan Wing Kei　DF: Leslie Chan Design Co. Ltd.

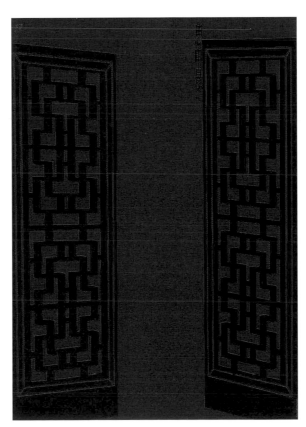

Process Black
PANTONE Process Blue

Process Black
PANTONE 364

Process Black
PANTONE 187

Poster 台湾デザイン協会展示会用ポスター　*Taiwan*
CL: Taiwan Poster Design Association　CD, AD, D: Leslie Chan Wing Kei　DF: Leslie Chan Design Co. Ltd.

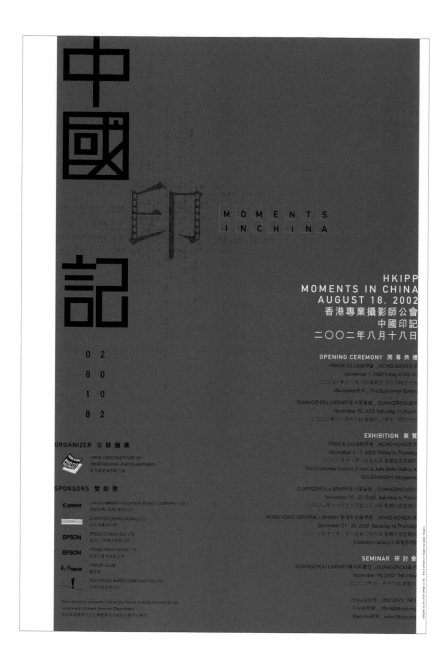

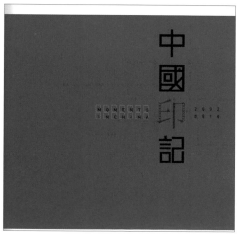

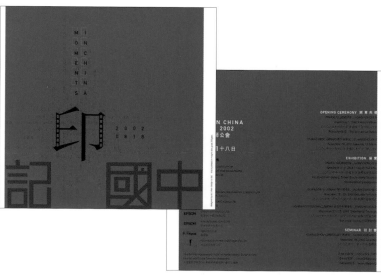

Process Black

PANTONE Red 032 U

Poster & Book Cover & Invitation Card 香港写真家協会 ポスター・ブックカバー・案内状　*Hong Kong*
CL: Hong Kong Institute of Professional Photographers　CD, AD, D: Eric Chan　AD, D: Francis Lee　DF: Eric Chan Design Co., Ltd.

白地に1&2色の
デザイン | 1&2 color design
on white paper | 075

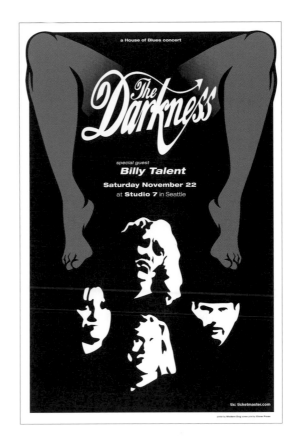

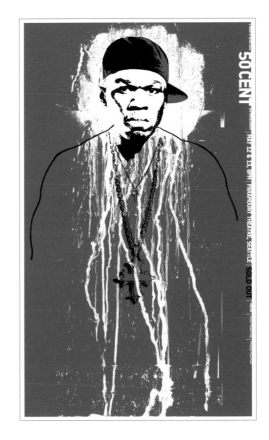

Concert Poster 音楽コンサートポスター *USA*
CL: House of Blues CD, AD, D, I: Robynne Raye DF: Modern Dog Design Co.

Concert Poster 音楽コンサートポスター *USA*
CL: House of Blues CD, AD, D, I: Junichi Tsuneoka DF: Modern Dog Design Co.

Concert Poster 音楽コンサートポスター *USA*
CL: House of Blues CD, AD, D, I: Junichi Tsuneoka DF: Modern Dog Design Co.

Concert Poster 音楽コンサートポスター *USA*
CL: House of Blues CD, AD, D, I: Michael Strassburger DF: Modern Dog Design Co.

PANTONE 245 U
PANTONE 294 U

Process Black
PANTONE 2755 U

Process Black
PANTONE 245 U

Process Black
PANTONE 179 U

Billboard 映画館ビルボード *Italy*
CL: Cineclub Il Raggio Verde   CD, DF: Enrico Coari

白地に1＆2色の
デザイン | **1&2 color design
on white paper** | 077

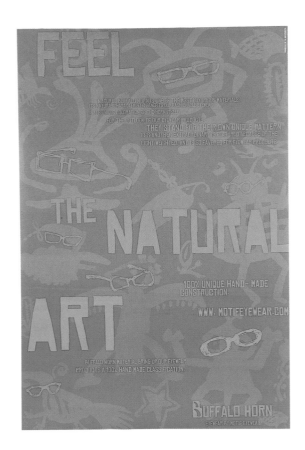

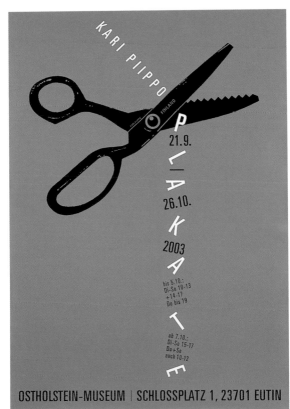

PANTONE 371 U
PANTONE 130 U

PANTONE 137 U
PANTONE 110 U

Process Black
PANTONE 146 U

Poster 眼鏡貿易会社イメージポスター　*Hong Kong*
CL: 4i Limited　AD, D, I: Joseph Leung　DF: Motakding Design

Poster 美術館ポスター　*USA*
CL: Ostholstein-Museum　AD, D Kari Plippo　DF: Kari Plippo Oy

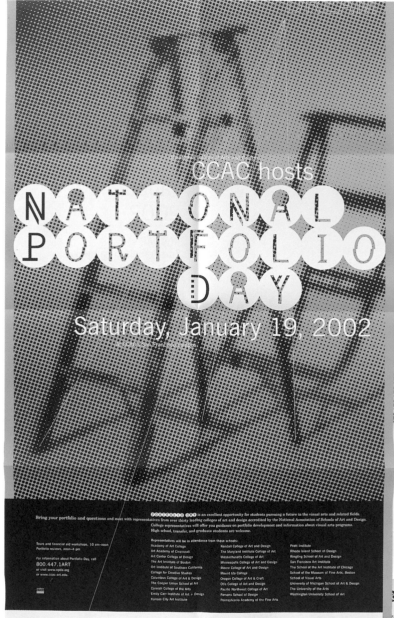

Process Black

PANTONE 382 U

Poster 大学キャンパスイベントのポスター *USA*

CL: California College of Arts and Crafts   AD, D: Bob Aufuldish   P: Luis Delgado   DF: Aufuldish & Warinner

Process Black

PANTONE 485 C

Flyer & Mailer 教育施設のフライヤー・DM *USA*
CL: California College of Arts and Crafts Institute   AD, D: Bob Aufuldish   I: Thom Faulders, Hajime Masubuchi, Beige Design   DF: Aufuldish & Warinner

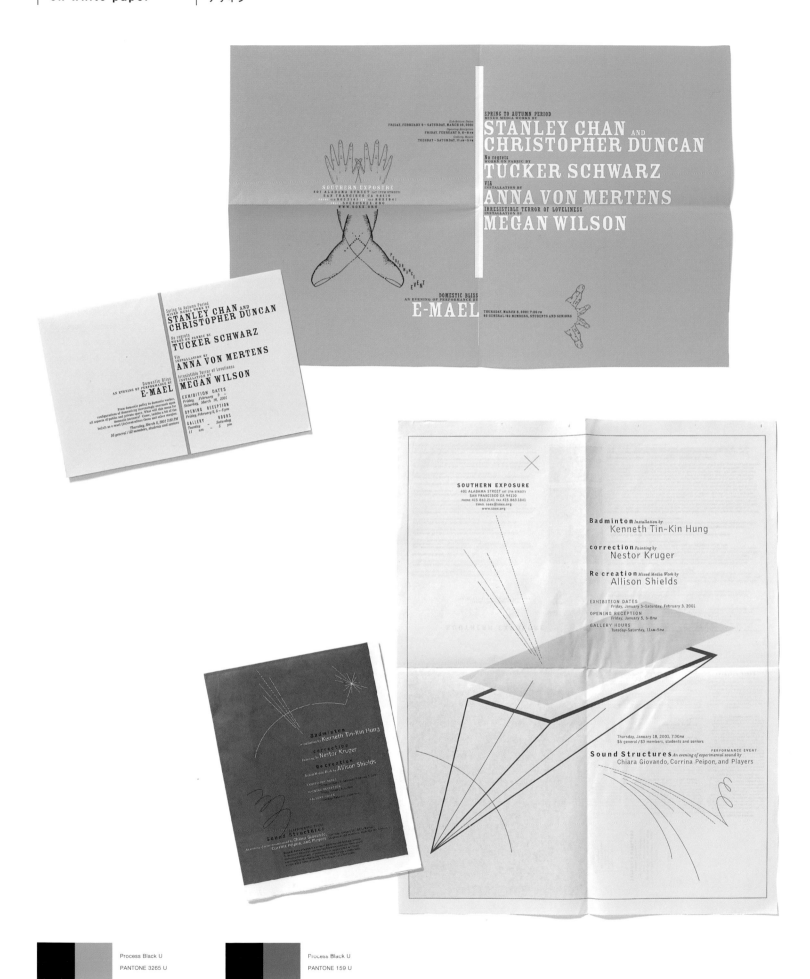

	Process Black U
	PANTONE 3265 U

	Process Black U
	PANTONE 159 U

Poster 美術展示会ポスター　*USA*
CL: Southern Exposure　D: Efrat Rafaeli　DF: Efrat Rafaeli Design

Newsletter & Poster 美術展示会ニュースレター・ポスター　*USA*
CL: Southern Exposure　D: Efrat Rafaeli　DF: Efrat Rafaeli Design

白地に1＆2色の
デザイン | 1&2 color design
on white paper | 081

Process Black

PANTONE 304 C

Poster 広告会社PR用ポスター *Hong Kong*
CL: Tupos Design Company   CD, D: Gabriel Tsang   AD, I: Iris Kwok   D: Orli Chow   DF: Tupos Design Company

 Process Black
PANTONE 583 U

 Process Black
PANTONE Orange 021 U

Poster & Invitation 美術館ポスター・案内状　*USA*
CL: Bellevue Art Museum　CD, AD: Kurt Wolken　D: Julie Schneider　DF: Wolken Communica

Music Program Folder 音楽スタジオ会社のプログラムフォルダー　*The Netherlands*
CL: Intro | in situ　CD, AD, D: J.J.F.G.Borrenberg　AD, DF: Stoere Binken Design

a   b   c   d

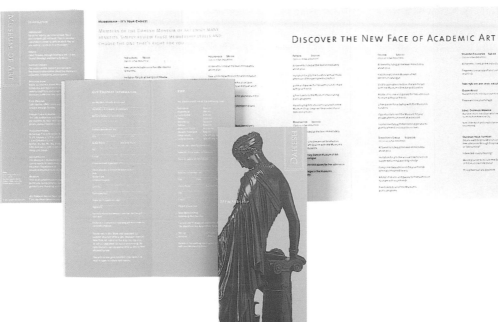

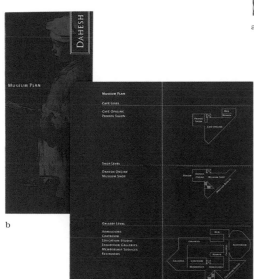

a

b   c

a   Process Black   PANTONE 611 C

b   Process Black   PANTONE 1807 C

c   Process Black   PANTONE Orange 021 C

d   Process Black   PANTONE 661 C

Pamphlet 美術館パンフレット   *USA*
CL: Dahesh Museum of Art   D: L. Richard Poulin, Brian Brindisi, Anna Crider   DF: Poulin + Morris

Process Black

Flyer, Business Card & Program 映画祭フライヤー・名刺・プログラム *Australia*
CL: Shorts Film Festival   CD, AD, D: Anthony De Leo   CD, AD: Scott Carslake   DF: Voice

白地に1＆2色の
デザイン | **1＆2 color design
on white paper** | 085

 Process Black

 PANTONE 213 U

Poster デザイン事務所ポスター　*Australia*
CL: Voice　CD, AD, D: Scott Carslake　/ Anthony De Leo　DF: Voice

Poster アパレルポスター　*Australia*
CL: Lotus　CD, AD: Anthony De Leo　CD, AD, D: Scott Carslake　DF: Voice

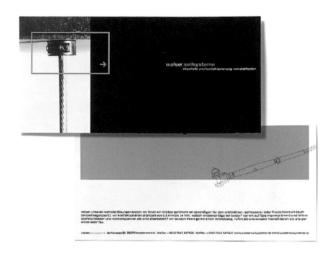

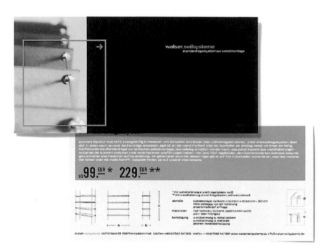

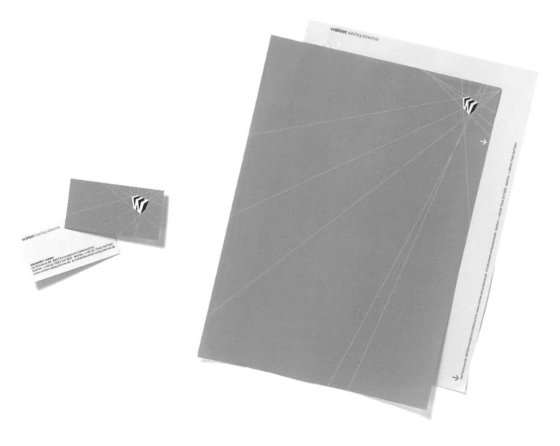

Process Black

PANTONE 137 U

Stationery ステーショナリー一式　*Germany*
CL: Walter　CD, AD, D, P, I: Kan Busche　DF: Graphic-o-Roma

白地に1＆2色の
デザイン | 1&2 color design
on white paper | 087

a | Process Black
PANTONE 3115 U

b | Process Black
PANTONE 116 U

c | Process Black
PANTONE Red 032 U

d | Process Black
PANTONE 361

Campaign 広告　*USA*　*a-c
CL: Big Brothers Big Sisters of Central Iowa　CD, AD, D: John Sayles　D: Som Inthalangsy　DF: Sayles Graphic Design

Poster & Direct Mail & Tent Card 図書館ポスター・DM・カード　*USA*　*d
CL: Brooklyn Public Library　CD, D: Graham Hanson　CW: Harvest Communications　DF: Graham Hanson Design

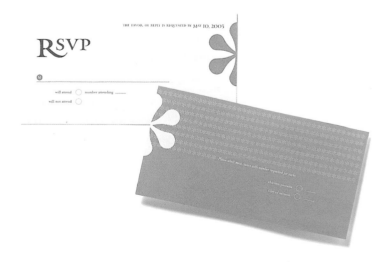

PANTONE 577 U
PANTONE 5415 U

Invitation 個人使用の招待状 *USA*
CL: David & Laura Satafia   CD, AD, D: David Salafia, Laura Salafia

Process Black

PANTONE 200 U

Invitation & Brochure 学校案内 *USA*

CL: Harvard Medical School CD, AD: Natalie Pangaro, Shannon Beer D: David Salafia DF: Pangaro Beer Design

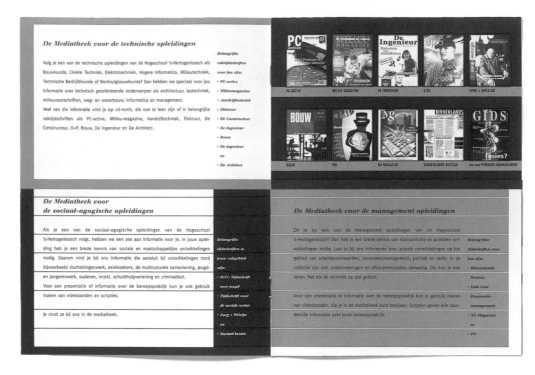

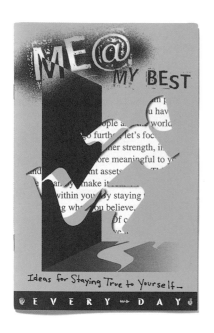

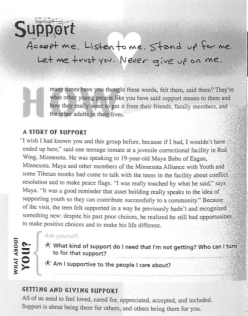

PANTONE Black 6 U
PANTONE 485 U 2X

Process Black
PANTONE 116 U

Small Book 小型本 *The Netherlands*
CL: Hoge School   CD, AD, D: Petra Janssen, Edwin Vollebergh   CD, AD, D, DF: Studio Boot

Booklet ブックレット *USA*
CL: Search Institute   CD, D, I: Brad Norr   DF: Brad Norr Design

Process Black
PANTONE 644 U

PANTONE 644 U
PANTONE 4485 U

Brochure 慈善団体ブローシャー　*USA*
CL: ALS Association of Oregon & SW Washington　D: Karen Wippich, Jon Wippich　DF: Dotzero Design

Direct Mail Brochure 慈善団体DM兼ブローシャー　*USA*
CL: ALS Association of Oregon & SW Washington　D: Karen Wippich, Jon Wippich　DF: Dotzero Design

a-1

a-2

b-1

b-2

a-1

PANTONE 5875 U
PANTONE 1935 U

a-2

PANTONE Cool Gray 11 U
PANTONE 122 U

b-1

PANTONE 123 U
PANTONE 443 U

b-2

PANTONE 232 U
PANTONE 463 U

Small Pamphlet Book 劇場パンフレット本 *The Netherlands*
CL: Leids Cabaret Festival   CD, AD, D: Petra Janssen, Edwin Vollebergh   P: Marcus Peters   CD, AD, D, I, DF: Studio Boot

白地に1＆2色の
デザイン | 1&2 color design
on white paper | 093

Renee van Bavel

De vorm van het soloprogramma van Renee van Bavel past in de lange traditie van het Nederlands cabaret; een aaneenschakeling van liedjes, verhalen en typeringen.

Het thema is ook niet nieuw, een jonge meid op zoek naar haar identiteit. Is er dan wel nieuws onder de zon? Renee vindt van wel. Als 3e-jaars aan de Koningstheaterakademie kent ze haar klassieken.

Zij beschouwt het als een compliment als u een glimp opvangt van de singer-songwriters die ze bewondert en de cabaretiers die ze een voorbeeld voor haar zijn.

Maar zij is pas tevreden als haar eigenheid afdoende doorklinkt.

TEKST EN MUZIEK: Renee van Bavel
REGIE: Anita Vinke Haag
MUZIKAAL ADVIES: Martijn Brouboart

**VOORRONDE
MAANDAG 11 FEBRUARI**

c-1

c-2

Schering en Inslag
'PARA'

Maten blijven maten voor het leven. Toch? Edo Berger, Thijs Niemantsverdriet, Joris van Wijk en musikant Jasper Rebel verkennen de grenzen van hun macht, en laten zich daarbij van hun slechtste kant zien. In 'Para' passeren goedkope grappen en een flinke dosis leedvermaak in hoog tempo de revue. Schering en Inslag dist elkaar, het publiek en de maatschappij. En dan moet er onherroepelijk ingegrepen worden. Toch?
www.scheringeninslag.nl

**VOORRONDE
MAANDAG 10 FEBRUARI**

d-1

d-2

c-1	PANTONE 812 U / PANTONE 606 U		
c-2	PANTONE 638 U / PANTONE 4495 U		
d-1	PANTONE 389 U / PANTONE 4495 U		
d-2	PANTONE 4635 U / PANTONE Rhodamine Red U		

a

b

Process Black

PE   PANTONE 877 U

a

b

Pamphlet Real Life Project パンフレット   *Japan*
CL, SB: Real Life Project リアル・ライフ・プロジェクト

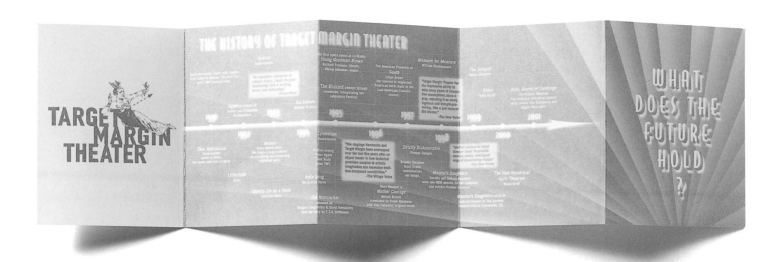

PE — PANTONE 877 U

Invitation 劇場案内状　*USA*
CL: Target Margin Theater　AD, D: Noah Scalin　DF: ALR Design

PANTONE 2955 U
PANTONE 5773 U

Concert Program 楽団プログラム用　*The Netherlands*
CL: Rotterdam Philharmonic Orchestra　CD, D: Arno Bauman　AD, I: Inge van der Ploeg　DF: Studio Bauman

a

b

c

a

Process Black
PANTONE 152 U

b

Process Black
PANTONE 312 U

c

Process Black
PANTONE 389 U

Brochure 学校案内 *USA* *a
CL: California College of Arts and Crafts   AD, D, P: Bob Aufuldish   I: Emily Aufuldish   DF: Aufuldish & Warinner

Brochure 学校案内 *USA* *b, c
CL: California College of Arts and Crafts   AD, D, P: Bob Aufuldish   DF: Aufuldish & Warinner

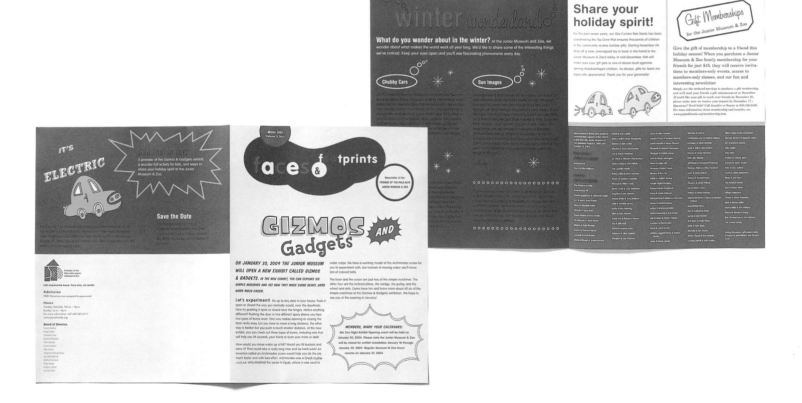

PANTONE 1655 U
PANTONE 314 U

PANTONE 212 U
PANTONE 364 U

Newsletter 児童博物館ニュースレター　*USA*
CL: Friends of Palo Alto Junior Museum and 200　D, I: Efrat Rafaeli　DF: Palo Alto Junior Museum - in House

白地に1&2色の
デザイン | 1&2 color design
on white paper | 099

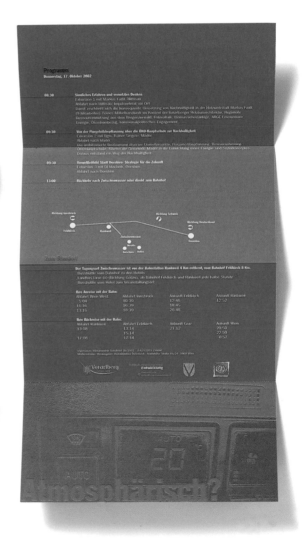

PANTONE 287 U

PANTONE 382 U

PANTONE 307 U

PANTONE 179 U

Brochure 児童博物館ブローシャー　*USA*
CL: Friends of Palo Alto Junior Museum and 200　D: Efrat Rafaeli　DF: Palo Alto Junior Museum - in House

Invitation プログラムの案内状　*Austria*
CL: Gemeinoe Zwischenwasser　CD: Sigi Ramoser　D: Sabine Sowieja　DF: Sagenvier Designkommunikation

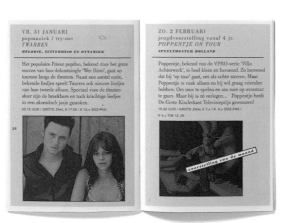

PANTONE 124 U
PANTONE 2735 U

PANTONE 2915 U
PANTONE 181 U

PANTONE 172 U
Process Black

Small Pamphlet Book 劇場パンフレット本 *The Netherlands*
CL: Theatre Kampen   CD, AD, D: Petra Janssen, Edwin Vollebergh   CD, AD, D, DF: Studio Boot

Process Black
PANTONE 2385 C

Process Black
PANTONE 1788 C

Process Black
PANTONE 368 C

PANTONE 282 C
PANTONE 2985 C

Process Black
PANTONE 1795 C

Process Black
PANTONE 136 C

PANTONE 2757 C
PANTONE 184 C

Process Black
PANTONE 1625 C

Movie Theatre Program Pamphlet 映画館上映プログラムパンフレット *Japan*
CL, SB: Kyoto Minami Theatre 京都みなみ会館

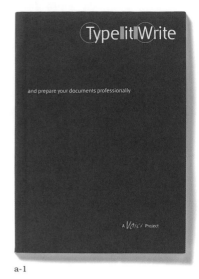

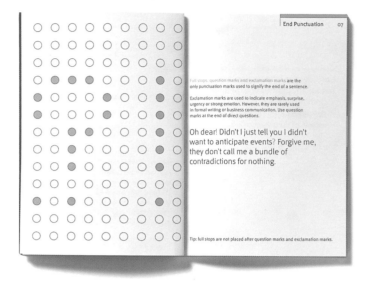

a-1

a-2

b

a-1 | PANTONE 5405 U
PANTONE 802 U

a-2 | Process Black
PANTONE 802 U

b | Process Black
PANTONE Red 032 C

Book(Cover) デザイン事務所PR本（カバー）　*Australia*　*a
CL: Voice　CD, AD, D: Scott Carslake　CD, D: Anthony De Leo　DF: Voice

Brochure ブローシャー　*Italy*　*b
CL: Borsani Comunicazione　CD, AD, D: Enrico Sempi　DF: Tangram Strategic Design

*エンボス＋スタンプ＋シール
Embossing + Stamp + Sticker Sheet

Process Black
PANTONE Orange 021 U

University Booklet 学校案内ブックレット *Germany*
CL: Hochschule Fur Kunste, University of the Arts Bremen D: Teacher: Eckhard Jung, Daniel Bastian, Jsabell Zirbeck, Stefan Bargstedt, David Lindemann

back

front

a

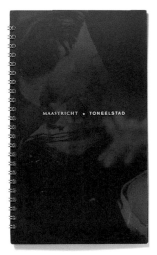

b-1

b-2

a

Process Black
PANTONE 395 U

b-1

PANTONE Black 4C
PANTONE Red 032 C

b-2

PANTONE Black 4C
PANTONE 8020 C

Brochure ブローシャー　*The Netherlands*
CL: KNZV Limburg　CD, AD, D: R.Verkaart　DF: Stoere Binken Design

Brochure 観光協会ブローシャー　*The Netherlands*
CL: VVV Maastricht　CD, AD, D: J.J.F.G.Borrenbergs　P: Joris Jan Bos, John Lambrichts, Carry Gisbertz, Danielle Amendt, Jo van Laar　DF: Stoere Binken Design

白地に1＆2色の
デザイン | 1＆2 color design
on white paper | 105

Process Black
PANTONE 397 U

Book 本 *Germany*
CL: Vaja E.V. Bremen   AD: Daniel Bastian, Uysses Voelker

Process Black

Fluorescent pink (≒PANTONE 806)

Magazine Cover 雑誌表紙 *France*
CL: Fairy Tale Magazine P: Anna Hankow, Jochen Braun DF: Vier5

白地に1＆2色の
デザイン | **1&2 color design
on white paper** | 107

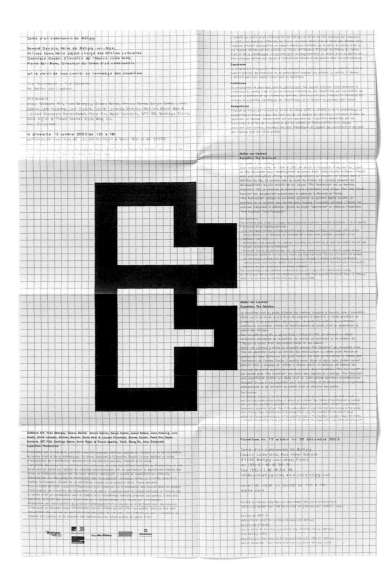

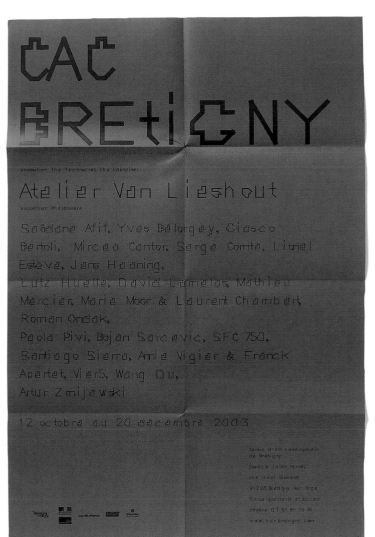

■ Process Black

■ PANTONE 2655 C

Poster, Flyer 美術館ポスター、美術館フライヤー　*France*
CL: Contemporary Art Centre Bretigny-sur-Orge　DF: Vier5

*表紙は3色を使用。
Front Cover uses 3 colors.

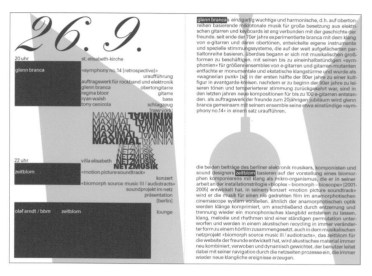

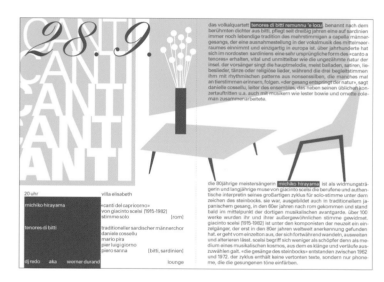

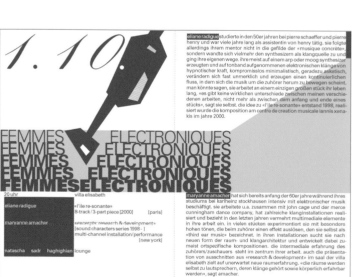

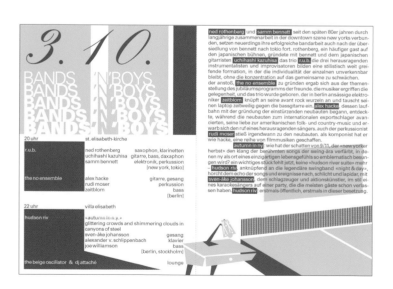

F	PE	PANTONE 804 U
		PANTONE 876 U

Brochure (Cover + Text) ブローシャー（カバー＋テキスト）　*Germany*
CL: Freunde Guter Musik　DF: Cyan

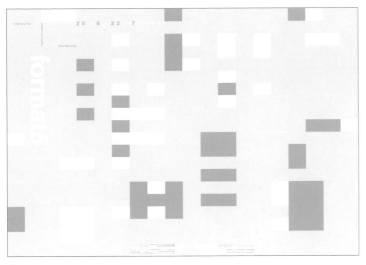

Cover

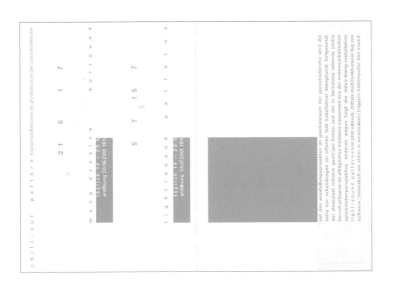

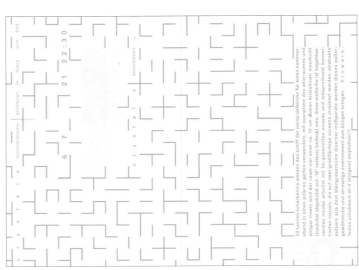

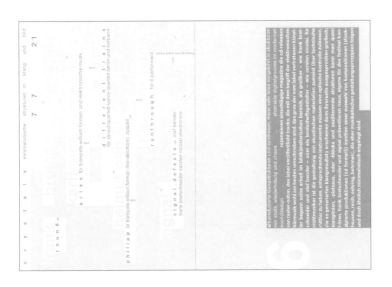

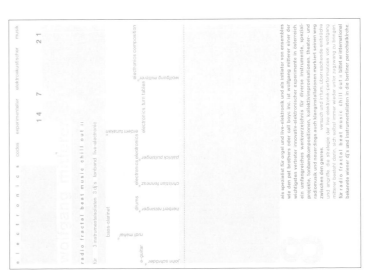

| F | PE | PANTONE 803 U |
| | | PANTONE 877 U |

Brochure (Cover + Text) ブローシャー（カバー＋テキスト）　*Germany*
CL: Format 5 - International Festival of Sound Art　DF: Cyan

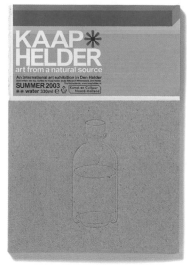

*エンボス
Embossing

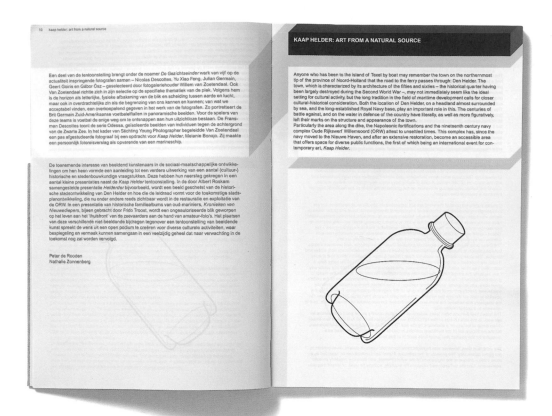

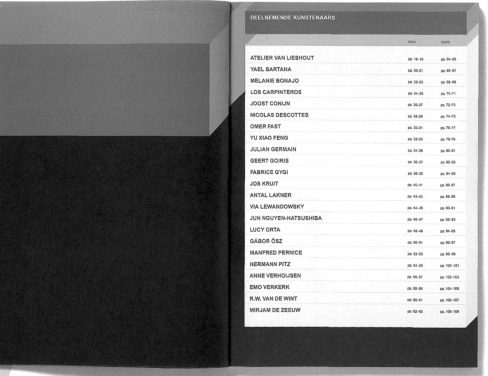

Process Cyan

PANTONE Reflex Blue C

Water & Brochure　ペットボトル・ブローシャー　*The Netherlands*
CL: Kunst & Kultuur　CD: Erik Kessels, Dave Bell　AD, D: Yuji Tokuda　P: Bas Odmes　DF: Kessels Kramer

Process Black

PANTONE Warm Red U

Newspaper 衣服販売会社の広報紙 *The Netherlands*
CL: Diesel　CD, AD, D: Erik Kessels　CD: Dave Bell　D, I: Anthony Burril　P: Carl de Keyzer　DF: Eric Hesen, Kessels Kramer

Process Black
Process Cyan

Brochure 携帯電話会社ブローシャー　*The Netherlands*
CL: Ben　CD, AD, D: Erik Kessels　CD: Dave Bell　P: Bert Teunissen, Lies Musch　DF: Kessels Kramer

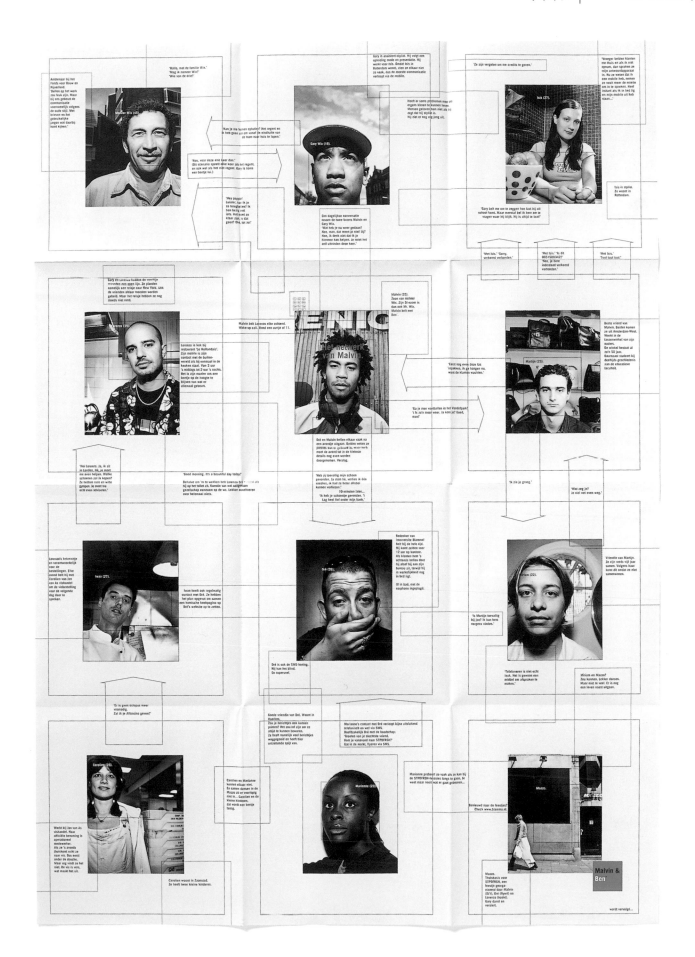

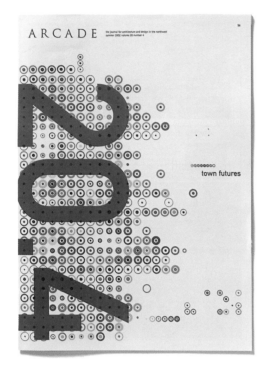

ARCADE

town futures

local focus

multiplied light: bullseye chandelier project
interviews by john cava | photographs by paul foster

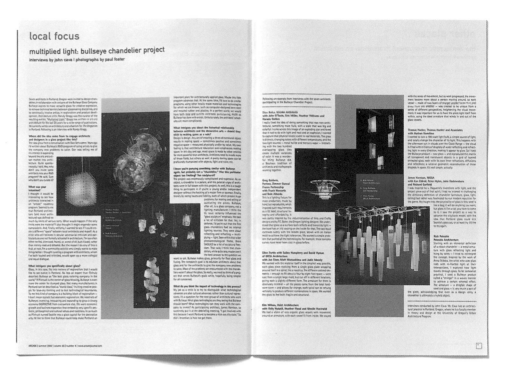

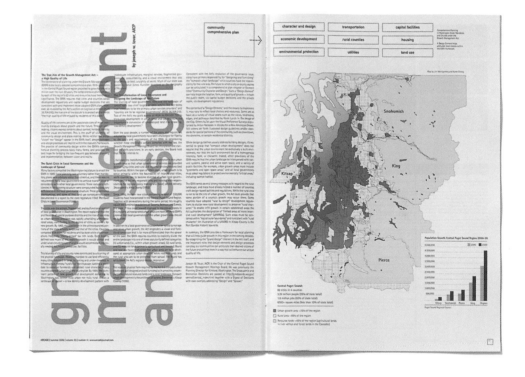

Process Black

PANTONE 3005 U

Magazine 公共団体発行の建築デザイン関連雑誌　*USA*
CL: Arcade Journal for Architecture and Design　D: Karen Cheng　DF: Cheng Design

john yeon in the land of influence | randy gragg

ARCADE

the idea
of regionalism

navin rawanchaikul's public proposition
by keith wallace

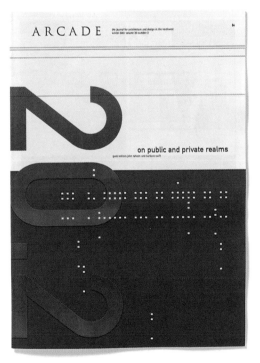

ARCADE

on public and private realms

Process Black
PANTONE 382 U

Process Black
PANTONE Warm Red U

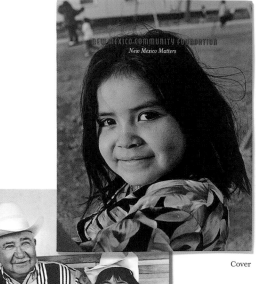

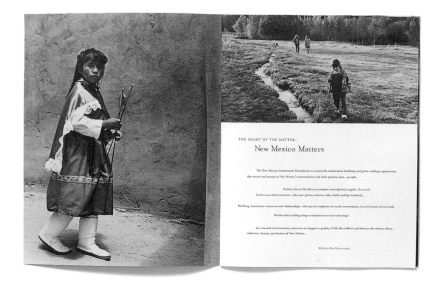

Cover

Case

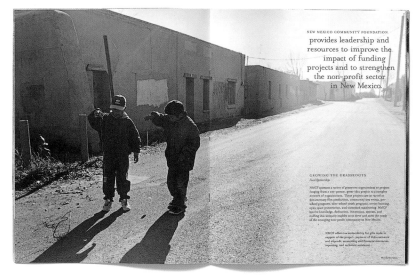

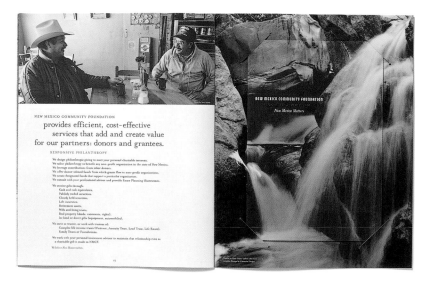

Process Black

PANTONE 471 C

Annual Report & Brochure 児童施設アニュアルレポート・ブローシャー *USA*

CL: New Mexico Community Foundation   AD: Brian Hurshman   D: Yvette Jones   P: Sam Adams, Don Usner   DF: Cisneros Design Inc.

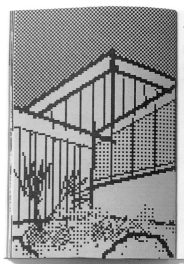

Timeless Structures
Prevailing in a Shifting Landscape

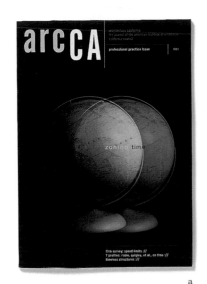

a

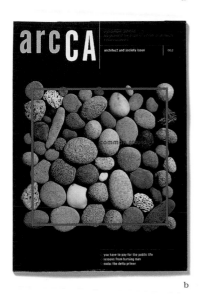

b

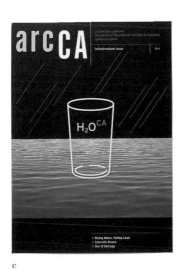

c

d

e

f

	Process Black	
a		PANTONE 549 C
b	Process Black	PANTONE 485 C
c	Process Black	PANTONE 0276 C
d	Process Black	PANTONE Rhodamine Red C
e	Process Black	PANTONE 7406 C
f	Process Black	PANTONE 3005 C

Journal Cover & Entire Issue 貿易機関発行の雑誌 *USA*
CL: American Institue of Architects California Council   AD, D, P: Bob Aufuldish   DF: Aufuldish & Warinner

Dürfen wir Sie herzlich willkommen heißen? Schließlich sind wir jetzt quasi Nachbarn. Denn wer in den besten Lagen der schönsten Städte wohnt, hat es zu Dahler & Company nicht weit. Wir sind die Spe- zialisten vor Ort. Die, die sich auskennen, die ihr Domizil gleich in Ihrer Nähe haben und die Ihnen jederzeit mit Rat und Tat beiseite stehen – soweit es Immobilien betrifft und gelegentlich auch einmal darüber hinaus. Schnell, diskret und kompetent.

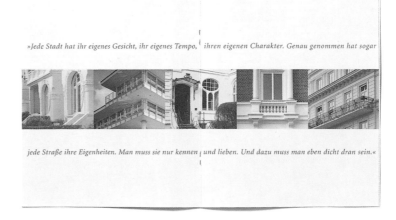

»Jede Stadt hat ihr eigenes Gesicht, ihr eigenes Tempo, ihren eigenen Charakter. Genau genommen hat sogar jede Straße ihre Eigenheiten. Man muss sie nur kennen und lieben. Und dazu muss man eben dicht dran sein.«

Process Black
PANTONE 158 U

Brochure 不動産会社ブローシャー　*Germany*
CL: Dalber + Company　CD, AD, D, I: Marius Fahrner　DF: Marius Fahrner Design

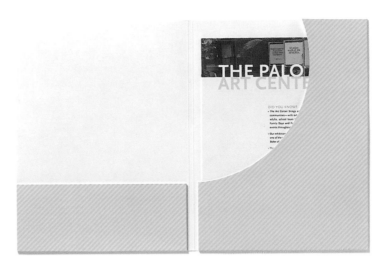

PANTONE 381 U

Process Black

Brochure & Data Sheet 芸術施設ブローシャー *USA*

CL: Palo Alto Art Center   CD: Elaine Tajima   AD: Thomas Whalen   D: Komal Dedhia   DF: Tajima Creative

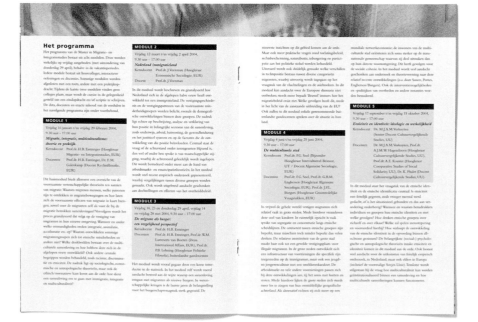

 Process Black
PANTONE 313 C

 Process Black
PANTONE 390 C

Brochure & Folder 学校案内・フォルダー *The Netherlands*
CL: Erasmus Plus   CD: Arno Bauman   D: Emmy van Harskamp   DF: Studio Bauman

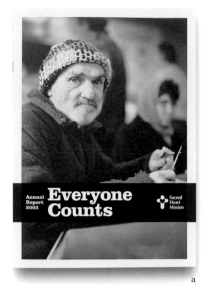

a

b

c

a

Process Black

PANTONE 485

b

Process Black

PANTONE 3145 U

c

Process Black

PANTONE 208 C

Annual Report 慈善活動アニュアルレポート　*Australia*　*a
CL: Sacred Heart Mission　CD, D: Andrew Hoyne　P: Marcus Struzina　DF: Hoyne Design

Folder & Brochure 教育施設 ブローシャー　*The Netherlands*　*b, c
CL: Segment　CD, D: Arno Bauman　DF: Studio Bauman

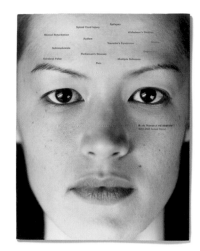

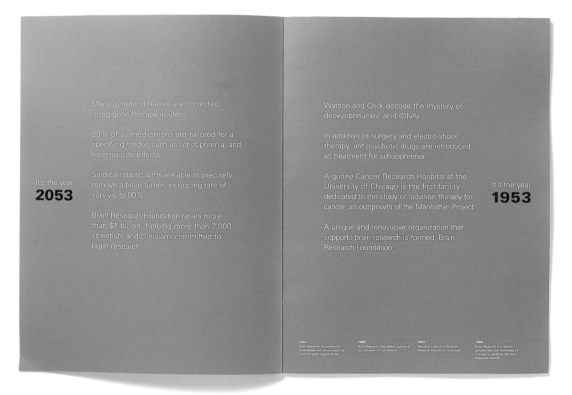

Many genetic diseases are corrected using gene therapy in utero.

80% of all medications are tailored for a specific disorder, such as schizophrenia, and have no side effects.

Surgical robotic arms are able to precisely remove a brain tumor, increasing rate of survival to 90%.

Brain Research Foundation raises more than $1 billion, funding more than 2,000 scientists and clinicians committed to brain research.

It's the year
2053

Watson and Crick decode the mystery of deoxyribonucleic acid (DNA).

In addition to surgery and electro-shock therapy, antipsychotic drugs are introduced as treatment for schizophrenia.

Argonne Cancer Research Hospital at the University of Chicago is the first facility dedicated to the study of radiation therapy for cancer, an outgrowth of the Manhattan Project.

A unique and innovative organization that supports brain research is formed: Brain Research Foundation.

It's the year
1953

In April 2003, the International Human Genome Sequencing Consortium announces the successful completion of the human genetic sequence.

Researchers at the University of Chicago utilize the new Core Genetics Research Facility to investigate fundamental questions relating to a variety of disorders, including cancer and Parkinson's disease.

Researchers use new DNA array technology to begin to track the genetic cause of schizophrenia.

Brain Research Foundation's total contributions toward the advancement of brain research are $25 million, including support for more than 400 young scientists and clinicians through its seed grant program.

It's the year
2003

PE	TOYO Black (≒ Process Black)
	TOYO 1035 (≒ PANTONE 8221 C)

Annual Report 慈善活動団体のアニュアルレポート　*USA*

CL: Brain Research Foundation　CD, AD, D: Kim Fry　CD: Steve Liska　D: Kristen Merry　P: Tom Maday　DF: Liska + Associates, Inc.

白地に1＆2色の
デザイン | **1＆2 color design
on white paper** | 123

CBOE*direct*® HyTS™

On June 12, 2003, the Chicago Board Options Exchange® (CBOE®) introduced CBOEdirect HyTS, a revolutionary hybrid trading system. CBOE is the first exchange to truly marry the speed and efficiency of screen-based trading with the liquidity and price discovery of a competitive, open outcry marketplace.

By launching CBOE*direct* HyTS, CBOE has created a unique trading model, unlike that of any other options exchange.

The robust technology encompassed in CBOEdirect HyTS combines the best features of screen-based trading and floor-based markets. By crafting a multi-faceted trading environment that combines the key elements of each, CBOE now offers customers and market makers a groundbreaking "best of both worlds" options marketplace.

In 2003, CBOE redefined how options are traded. **Here's how we did it.**
Chicago Board Options Exchange Annual Report 2003

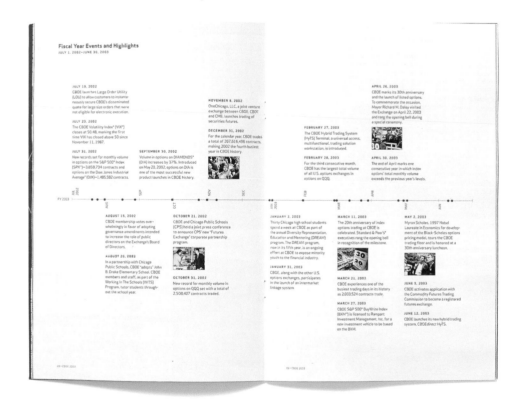

Fiscal Year Events and Highlights
JULY 1, 2002–JUNE 30, 2003

JULY 19, 2002
CBOE launches Large Order Utility (LOU) to allow customers to instantaneously secure CBOE's disseminated quote for large size orders that were not eligible for electronic execution.

JULY 23, 2002
The CBOE Volatility Index® (VIX®) closes at 50.48, marking the first time VIX has closed above 50 since November 11, 1987.

JULY 31, 2002
New records set for monthly volume in options on the S&P 500® Index (SPX®)—3,859,734 contracts and options on the Dow Jones Industrial Average® (DJX)—1,485,582 contracts.

SEPTEMBER 30, 2002
Volume in options on DIAMONDS® (DIA) increases by 37%. Introduced on May 20, 2002, options on DIA is one of the most successful new product launches in CBOE history.

NOVEMBER 8, 2002
OneChicago, LLC, a joint venture exchange between CBOE, CBOT and CME, launches trading of securities futures.

DECEMBER 31, 2002
For the calendar year, CBOE trades a total of 267,616,496 contracts, making 2002 the fourth busiest year in CBOE history.

FEBRUARY 27, 2003
The CBOE Hybrid Trading System (HyTS) Terminal, a universal access, multifunctional, trading solution workstation, is introduced.

FEBRUARY 28, 2003
For the third consecutive month, CBOE has the largest total volume of all U.S. options exchanges in options on QQQ.

APRIL 26, 2003
CBOE marks its 30th anniversary and the launch of listed options. To commemorate the occasion, Mayor Richard M. Daley visited the Exchange on April 22, 2003 and rang the opening bell during a special ceremony.

APRIL 30, 2003
The end of April marks one consecutive year in which index options' total monthly volume exceeds the previous year's levels.

FY 2003 | JUL 2002 | AUG | SEP | OCT | NOV | DEC | JAN 2003 | FEB | MAR | APR | MAY | JUN

AUGUST 19, 2002
CBOE membership votes overwhelmingly in favor of adopting governance amendments intended to increase the role of public directors on the Exchange's Board of Directors.

AUGUST 20, 2002
In a partnership with Chicago Public Schools, CBOE "adopts" John B. Drake Elementary School. CBOE members and staff, as part of the Working In The Schools (WITS) Program, tutor students throughout the school year.

OCTOBER 21, 2002
CBOE and Chicago Public Schools (CPS) hold a joint press conference to announce CPS' new "Futures Exchange" corporate partnership program.

OCTOBER 31, 2002
New record for monthly volume in options on QQQ set with a total of 2,508,407 contracts traded.

JANUARY 2, 2003
Thirty Chicago high school students spend a week at CBOE as part of the annual Diversity Representation, Education and Mentoring (DREAM) program. The DREAM program, now in its fifth year, is an ongoing effort at CBOE to expose minority youth to the financial industry.

JANUARY 31, 2003
CBOE, along with the other U.S. options exchanges, participates in the launch of an intermarket linkage system.

MARCH 21, 2003
CBOE experiences one of the busiest trading days in its history as 2,003,524 contracts trade.

MARCH 27, 2003
CBOE S&P 500® BuyWrite Index (BXM™) is licensed to Rampart Investment Management, Inc. for a new investment vehicle to be based on the BXM.

MARCH 11, 2003
The 20th anniversary of index options trading at CBOE is celebrated. Standard & Poor's® executives rang the opening bell in recognition of the milestone.

MAY 2, 2003
Myron Scholes, 1997 Nobel Laureate in Economics for development of the Black-Scholes options pricing model, tours the CBOE trading floor and is honored at a 30th anniversary luncheon.

JUNE 5, 2003
CBOE activates application with the Commodity Futures Trading Commission to become a registered futures exchange.

JUNE 12, 2003
CBOE launches its new hybrid trading system, CBOEdirect HyTS.

TOYO Black (≒PANTONE Black)
TOYO 0125 (≒PANTONE Warm Red C)

Annual Report 公共団体のアニュアルレポート *USA*
CL: Chicago Board Options Exchange   CD: Steve Liska   AD, D: Amy Hogan   P: Belden   DF: Liska + Associates, Inc.

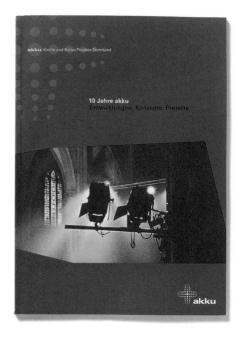

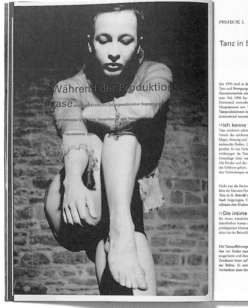

Process Black

PANTONE 1525 U

Broshure ブローシャー *Germany*

CL: Kirche Dortmund　CD: Rene Wynands, Silke Lohmann　D: Susanne Weiss　DF: Oktober Kommunikations Design GmbH

白地に1＆2色の
デザイン | 1＆2 color design
on white paper | 125

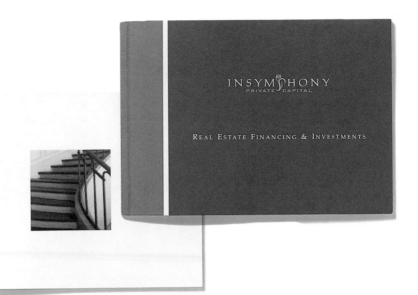

PE	PE	PANTONE 8561 U		Process Black
		PANTONE 871 U		PANTONE 286 C

Brochure 不動産投資会社ブローシャー　*USA*
CL: Insymphony Private Capital　CD, AD: Stan Evenson　D: Tricia Rauen　DF: Evenson Design Group

Brochure 慈善プログラム ブローシャー　*USA*
CL: United Way of Central New Mexico　CD, Writer: Sam Maclay　D: Tim McGrath　P: Michael Barley Studio　DF: Rick Johnson & Company

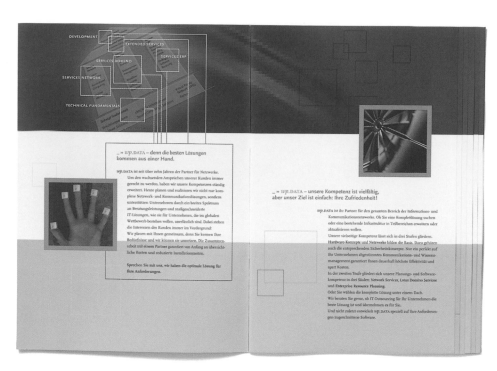

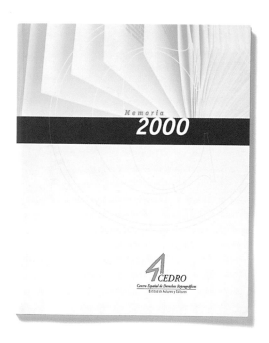

PE   PANTONE 877 U   PANTONE 285 U

PANTONE 173 C   PANTONE 429 C

Brochure ソフトウェア会社ブローシャー *Germany*
CL: wp. DATA   CD, AD, D: Herbert Rohsiepe   DF: graphische formgebung

Annual Report Book 公共施設アニュアルレポート *Spain*
CL: CEDRO   CD: Emilio Gil   D: Ingrid Forbord   DF: Tau Diseno

白地に1&2色の
デザイン | **1&2 color design
on white paper** | 127

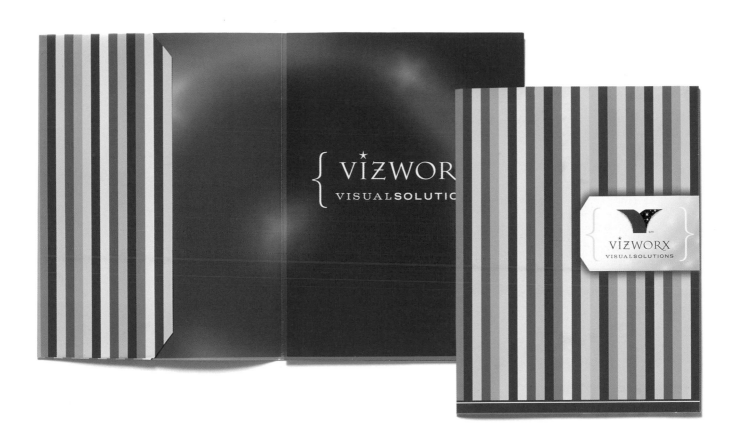

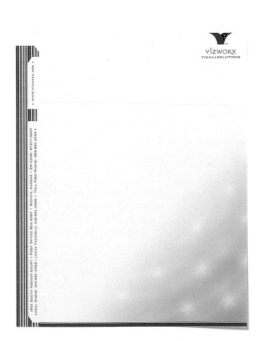

Process Black

PANTONE 2728 U

Corrospondence システム会社ステーショナリー一式 *USA*
CL: Vizworx CD: Bill Gardner AD: Brian Miller DF: Gardner Design

AGENDA
MAJ · 2002 · FRÅN JKL

HÅLL TUNGAN RÄTT I MUN
– OM ATT KOMMUNICERA CSR

I en tid då starka protester mot multinationella företag har blivit vardagsmat smyger sig nya aspekter in på företagsledningens agenda. Stora företag har fått erfara att värdeledda frågor som drivs av engagerade intressentgrupper är en högst reell och finansiell verklighet.

AGENDA
SEPTEMBER · 2003 · FRÅN JKL

NÄR ALLA SPRINGER MOT DÖRREN

Några framsynta aktieproffs började sälja av sina portföljer redan 1999. Men flertalet av aktieägarna behöll sina aktier en bra tid efter all-time high i mars 2000. När förhoppningarna grusades flydde allt fler börsen och till slut handlade det om ren evakuering från tillgångslaget.

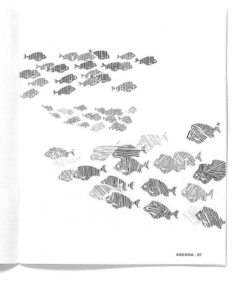

AGENDA
JUNI · 2003 · FRÅN JKL

ATT TILLTALA ETT KOLLEKTIV
AV INDIVIDUALISTER

För dagens unga finns de viktigaste auktoriteterna i den egna gruppen. När traditionella opinionsbildare tappar i betydelse blir vardagssamtalet viktigare.

PANTONE 137 U
PANTONE 357 U

Newsletter 広告会社PR用ニュースレター *Sweden*
CL: JKL   CD, AD, D: Helena Wahlman   DF: Wahlman Design

白地に1&2色の
デザイン | 1&2 color design
on white paper | 129

PANTONE 279 U
PANTONE 490 U

Process Black
PANTONE 805 C

Brochure ブローシャー *The Netherlands*
CL: KWH   D: Paul Vermijs, Masja van Deursen   DF: Tel Design

Annual Report 医療機関アニュアルレポート *Switzerland*
CL: Spitalregion Furstenland-Toggenburg   CD, AD: Lucia Frey   D: Manuela Pfrunder   P: Pascal Wuest   DF: Lucia Frey Design

a

b

a

Process Black
Process Yellow

b

Process Black
Process Magenta

Christmas Card & Flyer ギャラリーのクリスマスカード　*The Netherlands*
CL: Sirius　CD, AD, D: J.J.F.G.Borrenberg　DF: Stoere Binken Design

Flyer ギャラリーのパーティー用フライヤー　*The Netherlands*
CL: Sirius　CD, AD, D: J.J.F.G.Borrenberg　AD, DF: Stoere Binken Design

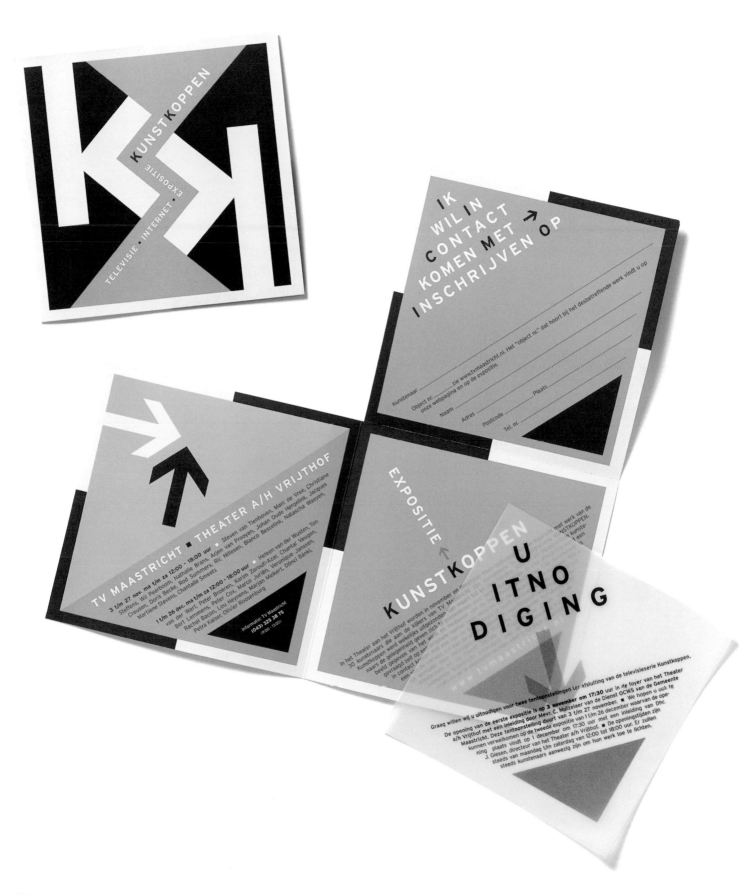

Process Black
PANTONE 375 U

Flyer テレビ局プロモーション用フライヤー   *The Netherlands*
CL: TV Maastricht   CD, AD, D: R.Verkaart   AD, DF: Stoere Binken Design

	F	Process Black
		PANTONE 804 C

Promotion Postcard デザイン事務所PR用ポストカード *Germany*
CL: 804 c Graphic Design   CD, P: Helge D. Rieder   CD: Oliver Henn   DF: 804 c Graphic Design

白地に1&2色の
デザイン | 1&2 color design
on white paper | 133

PANTONE 8223
PANTONE 8563

Staionery ビデオ販売店ステーショナリー　*Switzerland*
CL: Frequence Laser SA　CD, AD, D: Cristina Bolli Freitas　I: Laurent Bolli　DF: Bread and Butter

a

b

*エンボス
Embossing

c

		Process Black			Process Black			
a		PANTONE Warm Red U 2X	b		PANTONE 285 U	c		PANTONE 612 U

Invitation Card 招待状   *Italy*   *a
CL: Borsani Comunicazione   CD, AD, D: Enrico Sempi   DF: Tangram Strategic Design

Holiday Card デザイン事務所グリーティングカード   *USA*   *b
CL: Calori & Vanden-Eynden   AD: David Vanden-Eynden   D: Marisa Schulman   DF: Calori & Vanden-Eynden

Invitation Card 家具展示会招待状   *Mexico*   *c
CL: Nienkamper   CD, D: Vanessa Eckstein   Frances Chen   DF: Blok Design

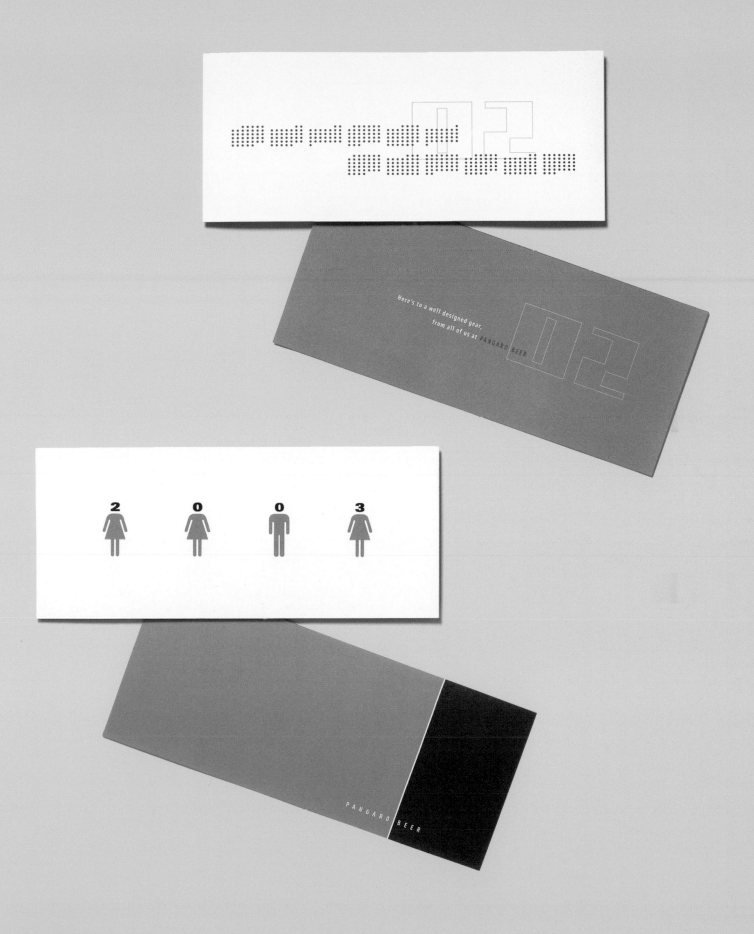

PANTONE 5493 U
PANTONE 180 U

Postcard デザイン事務所ポストカード *USA*
CL: Pangaro Beer Design   CD, AD: Natalie Pangaro, Shannon Beer   D: David Salafia   DF: Pangaro Beer Design

a	Process Black / PANTONE 551 C	
b	Process Black / PANTONE 5865 C	
c	Process Black / PANTONE 459 C	

Postcard 家具販売店PR用ポストカード *Austria*
CL: Tischlerei Engel Una Brotzge Furniture Firm   CD: Sigi Ramoser   D: Klaus Osterle   DF: Sagenvier Designkommunikation

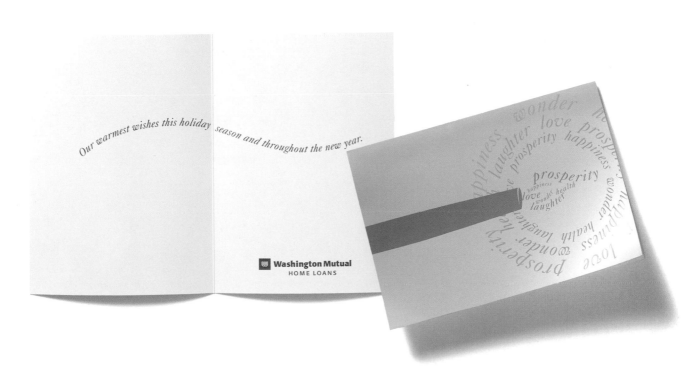

Process Black
PANTONE 180 U

PE   PE   PANTONE 877 U
            PANTONE 871 U

Invitation to Marriage Party 個人結婚式案内状 *Austria*
CL: Peter & Elisabeth Buchner   CD: Sigi Ramoser   D: Luis Rodriguez Lopez   DF: Sagenvier Designkommunikation

Holiday Card 金融会社グリーティングカード *USA*
CL: Washington Mutual, Inc.   CD: Elaine Tajima   AD: Thomas Whalen   D: Komal Dedhia   DF: Tajima Creative

Process Black
PANTONE 241 U

Postcard & Business Card PR用ポストカード・名刺　*Austria*
CL: Natur Kosmetic　CD: Sigi Ramoser　D: Marcel Schrattner　P: Nikolaus Walter　DF: Sagenvier Designkommunikation

白地に 1 & 2 色の
デザイン | 1 & 2 color design
on white paper | 139

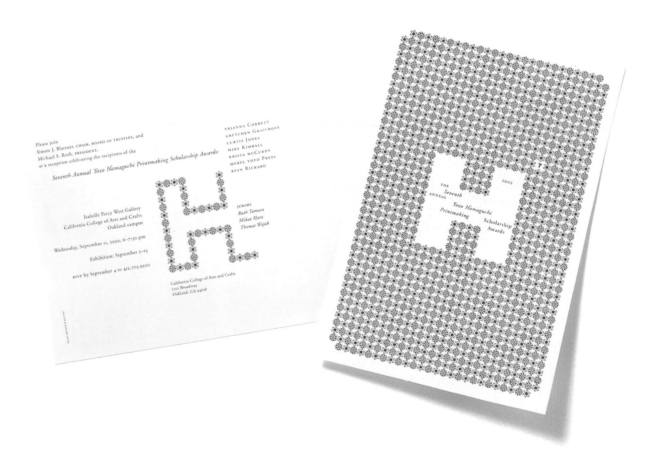

	PE	Process Black
		PANTONE 8004 C

| | | PANTONE 1817 U |

Postcard デザイナーポストカード *Germany*
CL: Helen D. Rieder   CD: Helge D. Rieder   DF: 804 c Graphic Design

Postcard 学校のポストカード *USA*
CL: California College of Arts and Crafts   AD, D: Bob Aufuldish   DF: Aufuldish & Warinner

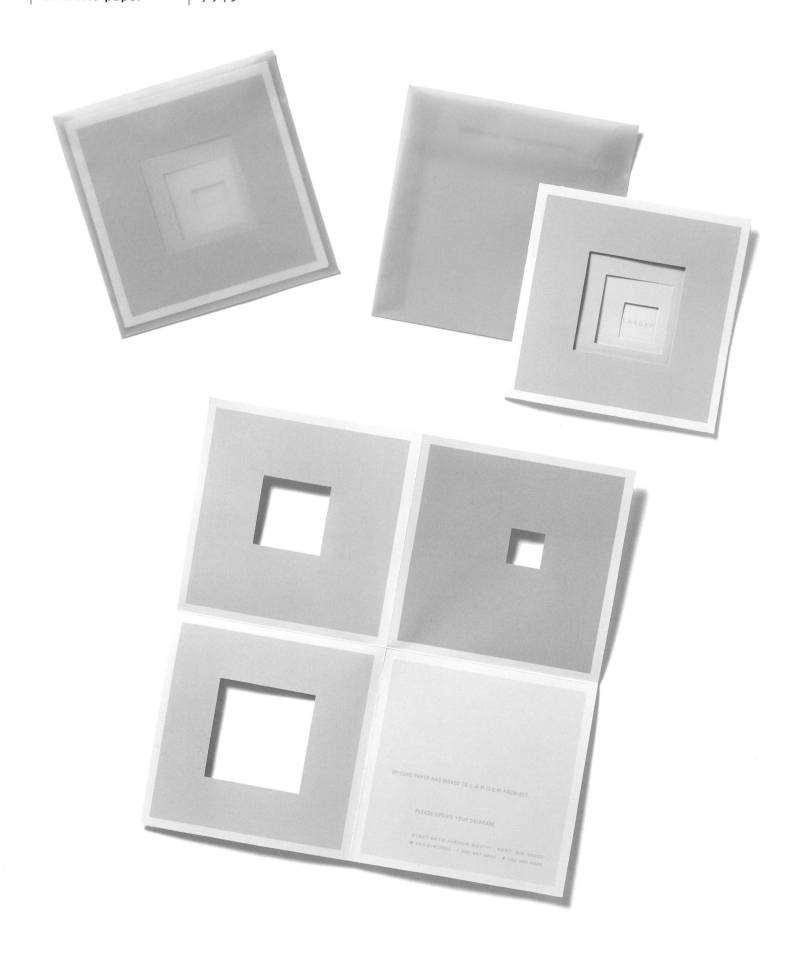

PANTONE 406 U
PANTONE 611 U

Moving Announcement Invitation 紙卸会社引っ越し告知案内状 *USA*
CL: Spicers Paper　D: Giorgio Davanzo　DF: Giorgio Davanzo Design

a

b

c

d

a　TOYO 0246 (≈PANTONE 376 U)
TOYO 0458 (≈PANTONE 2745 U)

b　TOYO 0091 (≈PANTONE 185 2X)
TOYO 0230 (≈PANTONE 396 U)

c　TOYO 0451 (≈PANTONE 661 U)
TOYO 0162 (≈PANTONE 123 U)

d　PANTONE Orange 021 U
PANTONE 877 U

Invitation　ホテル案内状　*USA*　*a-c
CL: Hotel 71　CD, AD, D: Steve Liska　D: Brian Graziano　DF: Liska + Associates, Inc.

Invitation Card　ソフトウェア会社イベント案内　*Hong Kong*　*d
CL: SP Consulting Limited　AD, D: Joseph Leung　DF: Motakding Design

a
PANTONE 116 U
PANTONE 7509 U

b
PANTONE 335 U
PANTONE Rubine Red U

c
PANTONE Rubine Red U
PANTONE 3135 U

d
Process Black
PANTONE 185 U 2X

Sales Announcement Direct Mail セール案内DM   *Japan   *a-c
CL: national standard ナショナルスタンダード   AD, D: Atsuki Kikuchi 菊池敦己   DF: Bluemark Inc. (株)ブルーマーク

Exhibition Direct Mail 「家紋展」案内DM   *Japan   *d (実際は3色で表現 actual works uses 3 colors)
CL: oeuf GALLERY ウフギャラリー   CD: Yoko Omori 大森伃佑子   AD, D: Atsuki Kikuchi 菊池敦己   DF: Bluemark Inc. (株)ブルーマーク

白地に1＆2色の
デザイン | 1&2 color design
on white paper | 103

Process Cyan

Stationery ウェブデザイン会社ステーショナリー *Switzerland*
CL: Netface SA CD, AD, D: Cristina Bolli Freitas I: Laurent Bolli DF: Bread and Butter

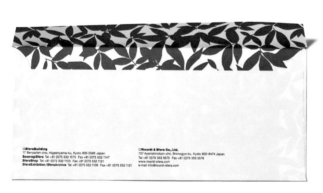

Process Black
PANTONE 364 U

*

Process Black
PANTONE 543 U

Graphic Identity ステーショナリー一式　*Sweden*
CL: Ricordi & Sfera　CD, AD, D: Markus Mostrom　DF: Markus Mostrom Design

白地に1＆2色の
デザイン | 1&2 color design
on white paper | 105

PANTONE 180 U
PANTONE 7500 U

*表面のみ4色使用
uses 4 color

Corrospondence 美容室ステーショナリー *USA*
CL: Modern Salon   CD: Bill Gardner   AD: Brian Miller   D: Zach Labrayere   DF: Garner Design

白地に1＆2色の
デザイン | **1＆2 color design
on white paper** | 107

Stationery 広告会社ステーショナリー　*Switzerland*
CL: Bread and Butter　CD, AD, D: Cristiana Bolli Freitas　I: Laurent Bolli　DF: Bread and Butter

a

b

b

a

a

c

a   PANTONE 9536 U
PANTONE 7505 U

b   PANTONE 7599 U
PANTONE 7505 U

c   PANTONE 9536 U
PANTONE 7599 U

Stationery 映像会社ステーショナリー一式   *Mexico*
CL: Distrito Films   CD, D: Vanessa Eckstein   DF: Blok Design

白地に1＆2色の
デザイン | **1&2 color design
on white paper** | 149

 a   PANTONE 545 U

 b   PANTONE 549 U

 c   PANTONE 548 U

Stationery ステーショナリー一式   *Mexico*
CL: Steam   CD, D: Vanessa Eckstein   D: Frances Chen   DF: Blok Design

a

b

c

d

 a Process Black
PANTONE 312 U

 b Process Black
PANTONE Orange 021 U

 c Process Black
PANTONE 225 U

 d Process Black
PANTONE 382 U

Letterheads & Postcards 大学のレターヘッド・ポストカード *USA*
CL: California College of Arts and Crafts   AD, D, P: Bob Aufuldish   DF: Aufuldish & Warinner

白地に1 & 2色の
デザイン | 1&2 color design
on white paper | 151

		Process Black	
a		Process Black	PANTONE 649 U
b		Process Black	PANTONE 460 U
c		Process Black	PANTONE 635 U
d		Process Black	PANTONE 630 U
e		Process Black	PANTONE 5305 U
f		Process Black	PANTONE 650 U
g		Process Black	PANTONE 4675 U
h		Process Black	PANTONE 5865 U

Postcard 教育プログラム告知用ポストカード　*USA*
CL: California College of Arts and Crafts Office of Enrollment Services　AD, D, P: Bob Aufuldish　DF: Aufuldish & Warinner

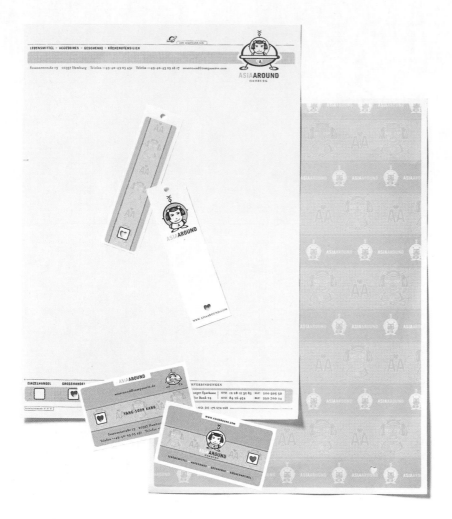

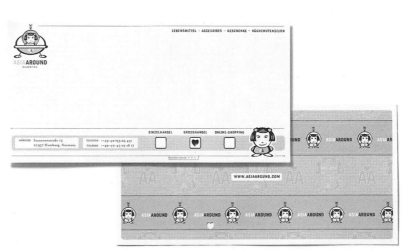

PANTONE 698 U
PANTONE 175 U

Stationery ステーショナリー *Germany*
CL: Asia Around   CD, AD, D, I: Marius Fahrner   DF: Marius Fahrner Design

白地に1＆2色の
デザイン | 1&2 color design
on white paper | 153

PANTONE 605 U
PANTONE 267 U

a

PANTONE Red 032 U
PANTONE 116 U

b

PANTONE Red 032 U
PANTONE Process Blue U

c

PANTONE 267 U
PANTONE 5773 U

d

Letterhead レターヘッド *USA* *a-c
CL: Outside the Box CD, AD, D: John Sayles D: Som Inthalangsy DF: Sayles Graphic Design

Letterhead レターヘッド *USA* *d
CL: The Home Connection CD, AD, D: John Sayles D: Som Inthalangsy DF: Sayles Graphic Design

a

b

c

d

a | Process Black / Process Cyan

b | Process Black / Process Magenta

c | Process Black / Process Yellow

d | Process Black

Letterhead レターヘッド　*The Netherlands*
CL: Drukzaken　D: Eugene Heijblorn, Anika Klevering　DF: Tel Design

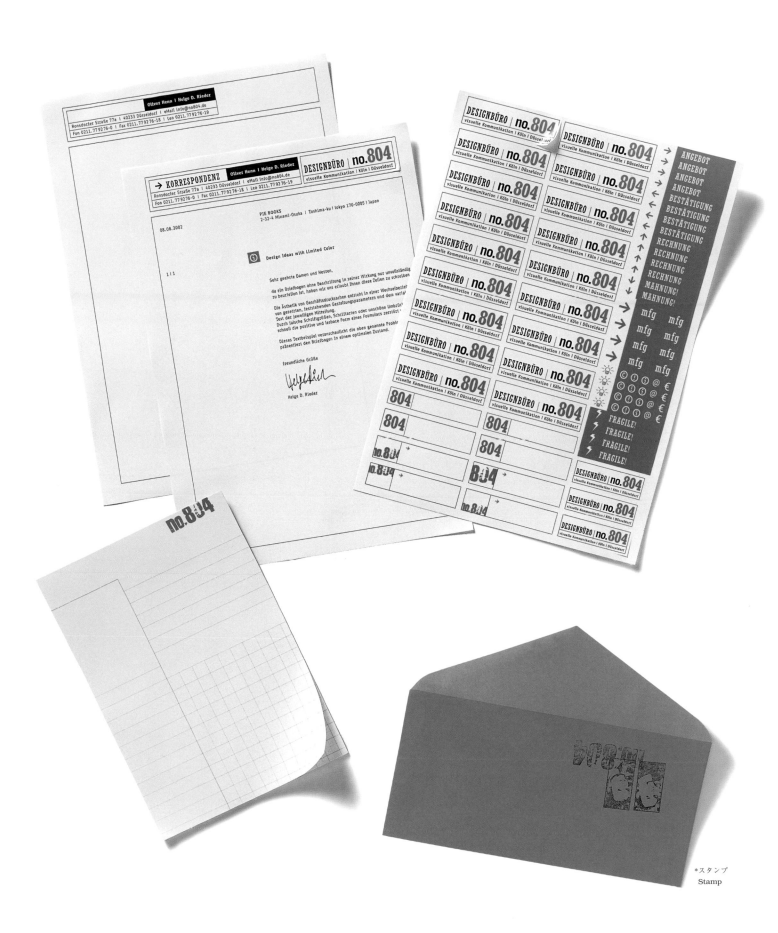

*スタンプ
Stamp

F   Process Black
PANTONE 804 C

Stationery デザイン事務所ステーショナリー　*Germany*
CL: Design Buro no. 804　CD: Helge D. Rieder, Oliver Henn　DF: 804 c Graphic Design

front

back

PANTONE 1665 U

PANTONE 404 U

Letterhead Package 広告協会レターヘッド *USA*
CL: New Mexico Advertising Federation   CD, Writer: Sam Maclay   D: Tim McGrath   DF: Rick Johnson & Company

白地に1＆2色の
デザイン | 1&2 color design
on white paper | 157

a

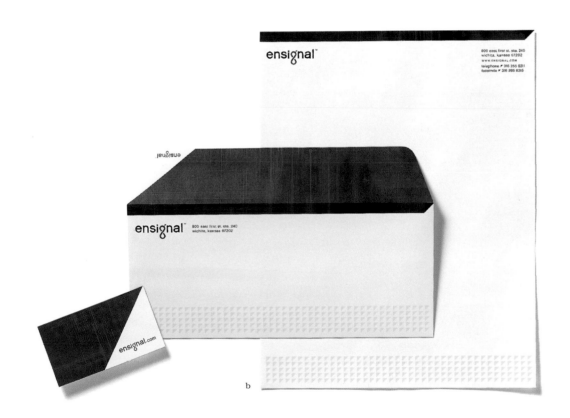

b

a
PANTONE Black 2 U
PANTONE 158 U

b
Process Black
PANTONE Red 032 U

Stationery 店舗デザイン会社ステーショナリー一式　*USA*
CL: Loopworx　D: Glorgio Davanzo　DF: Glorgio Davanzo Design

Corrospondence 携帯電話販売会社ステーショナリー　*USA*
CL: E Signal　CD: Bill Gardner　AD: Brian Miller　DF: Gardner Design

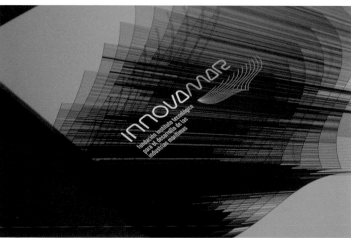

Process Black

PANTONE 2995 C

Label (Stationery) スペイン科学省ステーショナリー   *Spain*

CL: Innovamar Foundation   CD: Emilio Gil   AD: Jorge Garcia   DF: Tau Diseno

Business Card 医療機関施設 名刺 *USA* *a
CL: synexis cg　CD, AD, D: Wing Chan　DF: Wing Chan Design, Inc.

Business Card デザイン会社名刺 *Brazil* *b
CL: Antonio Marcio Rolla Guerra　CD, AD, D: Antonio Marcio Rolla Guerra　DF: Evenson Design Group

Business Card 個人名刺 *The Netherlands* *c
CL: Arno Pareja　D: Kees Wagenaars　DF: CASE

Business Card テクノロジー会社 名刺 *Italy* *d
CL: Morse srl　CD, AD, D: Andrea Greco　DF: Greco Design Studio

a　PANTONE 382 U / PANTONE Cool Grey 8 U

b　PANTONE Orange 021 C

c　PANTONE 398 U / PANTONE 222 U

d　PANTONE 116 U / PANTONE 280 U

back

■	PE	Process Black	
		PANTONE 877 C	
■		Process Black	

Stationery デザイン事務所ステーショナリー *Switzerland*
CL: Dance Function   CD, AD, D: Cristina Bolli Freitas   I: Laurent Bolli   DF: Bread and Butter

Business Card デザイン事務所名刺 *USA*
CL: Julie Rosen   CD, DF: Julie Rosen

白地に 1 & 2 色の
デザイン | 1&2 color design
on white paper | 161

a

Jackie Lu

Faces Esthetic & Beauty Spa
phone. 905.763.7785

155 East Beaver Creek Rd., Unit 21-22
Richmond Hill, Ontario L4B 2N1
www.facescanada.com

顔妝

b

Celia So

Faces Make-up Studio & Bridal Boutique
phone. 905.764.3066 | 905.764.8432

155 East Beaver Creek Rd., Unit 21-22
Richmond Hill, Ontario L4B 2N1
www.facescanada.com

顔妝

c

Quenise Lau

Faces Esthetic & Beauty Spa
phone. 905.763.7785

155 East Beaver Creek Rd., Unit 21-22
Richmond Hill, Ontario L4B 2N1
www.facescanada.com

顔妝

d

大
dai
dai

Fusako Miyakawa
宮川 房子

DAIDAI
FUTURE PLANNING PARTNERS
Piazza Castello 23
20121 Milano, Italy
T +39 02 89 289 720 (reception)
T +39 02 89 289 722 (direct)
F +39 02 89 289 724
fusako@futureplanningpartners.com

a Process Black PANTONE 5787 U

b Process Black PANTONE 466 U

c Process Black PANTONE 536 U

d PANTONE 233 U PANTONE 130 U

Business Card ブライダル施設会社名刺 *Canada*
CL: Faces Make-up Studio & Bridal Boutique & Faces Esthetic & Beauty Spa   CD, AD, D: Ivy Wong   DF: Splash Interactive Ltd.
Business Card 名刺 *Italy*
CL: Dai Dai   CD: Enrico Sempi   AD, D: Abotonella Trevisan   DF: Tangram Strategic Design

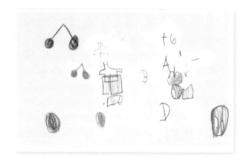

＊作品の裏面にはそれぞれがイラストを描けるようになっている。
Illustration can be drawn on the back.

Process Black
PANTONE 5523

Stationery 学校のステーショナリー　*USA*
CL: Volksschule Lochad　CD, AD: Stefan Sagmeister　D: Matthias Ernstberger　DF: Sagmeister Inc.

白地に1＆2色の
デザイン | 1&2 color design
on white paper | 163

a | Process Black
PANTONE 5487

b | Process Black
PANTONE 544 U

Business Card ミュージシャン名刺 *USA*
CL: Lou Reed   CD, AD: Stefan Sagmeister   D: Matthias Ernstberger   DF: Sagmeister Inc.

Business Card 個人名刺 *USA*
CL: Pete Heiberger   AD, D, P: Noah Scalin   DF: ALR Design

Process Black

PANTONE 139 U

Stationery インターネットカード会社ステーショナリー   *The Netherlands*

CL: DCC   CD, AD: Erik Kessels   CD: Dave Bell   AD, D, I: Krista Rozema   I: Stang   DF: Kessels Kramer

白地に1&2色の
デザイン | **1&2 color design
on white paper** | 165

a

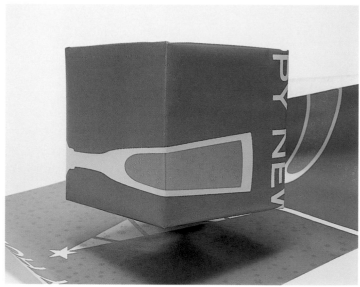

b

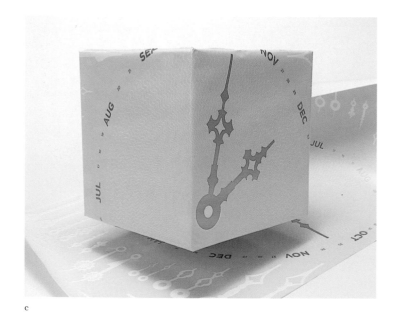

c

d

a

PANTONE 877 U
PANTONE Orange 021 U

b

PANTONE 877 U
PANTONE 646 U

c

PANTONE 877 U
PANTONE 128 U

d

PANTONE 877 U
PANTONE 7427 U

Wrapping Paper デザイン事務所使用の包装紙 *USA*
CL: Hornall Anderson Design Works, Inc.   D: Sonja Max, Henry Yiu, Kris Delaney   DF: Hornall Anderson Design Works, Inc.

白地に1＆2色の
デザイン | 1&2 color design
on white paper | 167

F		PANTONE 805 U
		Process Black

F	T	PANTONE 805 U
*		Thermography

Stationery 芸術学校ステーショナリー *The Netherlands*
CL: Sint Lucas   CD, AD: Erik Kessels   D, I: Eric Hesen   DF: Eric Hesen, Kessels Kramer

 PANTONE Warm Red U

 Process Black / Process Yellow

 PANTONE 300 U

 PANTONE 348 U

Brochure 衣服販売会社カレンダー型ブローシャー *The Netherlands*
CL: Diesel CD, AD: Erik Kessels CD: Dave Bell D: Julian Morey P: Finlay Mackay DF: Kessels Kramer

白地に1&2色の
デザイン | **1&2 color design
on white paper** | 169

front

back

Process Black

Process Yellow

Brochure 劇団ブローシャー *The Netherlands*
CL: Shockheaded Peter   CD, AD: Erik Kessels   P: Dodd Miller   DF: Kessels Kramer

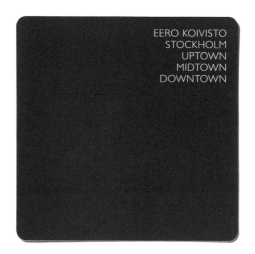

EERO KOIVISTO
STOCKHOLM
UPTOWN
MIDTOWN
DOWNTOWN

EERO KOIVISTO
STOCKHOLM
ORBIT

MÁRTEN CLAESSON
EERO KOIVISTO
OLA RUNE
STOCKHOLM
CORNFLAKE

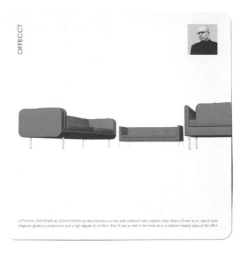

*様々な色のカタログが筒式のフォルダー内に収められている。
Different colored catalog is stocked inside the Box folder.

 PANTONE Red 032 C   PANTONE 368 C   PANTONE 3005 C

Box / Catalog presenting new furniture 家具カタログ   *Sweden*
CL: OFFECCT   CD, AD, D: Markus Mostrom   D: Rikard Ahlberg   DF: Markus Mostrom Design

白地に1＆2色の
デザイン | **1&2 color design
on white paper** | 171

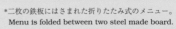

＊二枚の鉄板にはさまれた折りたたみ式のメニュー。
Menu is folded between two steel made board.

	PE	Process Black
		PANTONE 877 U

Menu レストラン メニュー *USA*
CL: The Spartan   CD: Bill Gardner   AD: Brian Miller   D: Elisabeth Owens   DF: Gardner Design

front

front

front

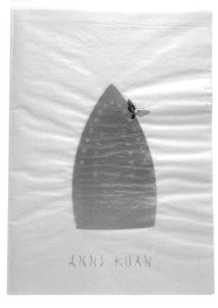
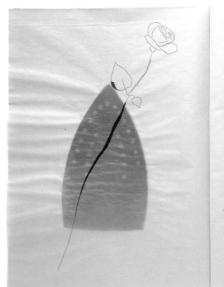

*用紙にアイロンでこげ跡がつくようにプレスされている。
Iron is pressed on to leave it's mark.

Process Black

Invitation アパレルイベント案内状　*USA*
CL: Anni Kuan　CD, AD: Stefan Sagmeister　D: Matthias Ernstberger　DF: Sagmeister Inc.

白地に１＆２色の
デザイン | **1 & 2 color design
on white paper** | 173

back

back

back

front

back

*4色使用
uses 4 colors

		Process Black			PANTONE 469 U
		PANTONE Red 032 U			PANTONE 650 U

Beermats コースター   *The Netherlands*
CL: Ascrum Rugby Club   CD: Erik Kessels   AD, D, I: Karen Heuter   DF: Kessels Kramer

Promotional Giveaway Coasters デザイン事務所PR用コースター   *USA*
CL: Dotzero Design   D, I: Karen Wippich, Jon Wippich   DF: Dotzero Design

白地に1＆2色の
デザイン | 1&2 color design
on white paper | 175

a

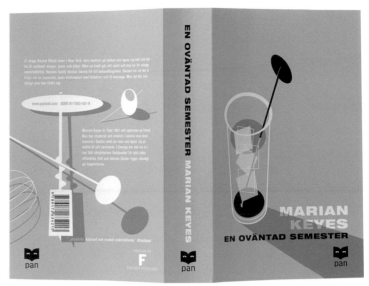

b

c

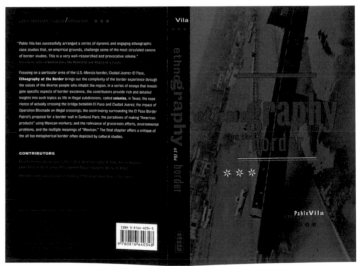

d

a

Process Black

PANTONE 212 U

b

Process Black

PANTONE 338 U

c

PANTONE 1915 C

PANTONE 2756 C

d

PANTONE 805 C

PANTONE 5467 C

Book Cover ブックカバー *Sweden* *a, b
CL: PAN Norstedts   D, I: Jonas Bergstrand   DF: Jonas Bergstrand Grafisk Design AB

Book Cover ブックカバー *USA* *c, d
CL: University of Minnesota Press   D: Efrat Rafaeli   DF: Efrat Rafaeli Design

a

b

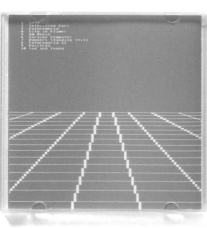

c

a		PANTONE Black
		PANTONE 151 C

b		Process Black
		Process Cyan

c	F	PANTONE 802 C

CD Cover CDジャケット *USA* *a, b
CL: The Real Diego/ What Else? Records   CD, AD, D, P: Andy Mueller   DF: Ohio Girl Design

CD Cover CDジャケット *USA* *c
CL: Trans Am/ Thrill Jockey Records   CD, AD, D, I: Andy Mueller   DF: Ohio Girl Design

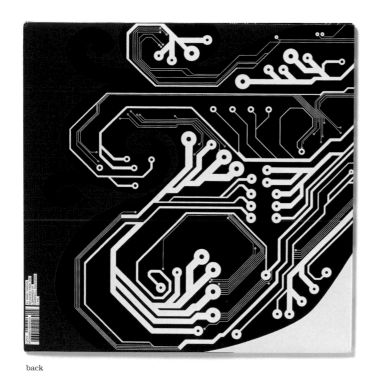

back

front

front

back

Process Black

PANTONE 485 C

Process Black

PANTONE 397 C

Record LP Sleeves レコードジャケット *UK*
CL: Lo Recordings   CD, AD, D, I: Kjell Ekhorn, Jon Forss   DF: Non-Format

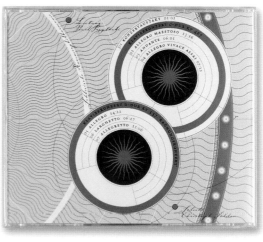

back

			Process Black				PE		PANTONE 872 C

 Process Black / PANTONE 305 C

 PE / PANTONE 872 C / PANTONE 295 C

CD Packege CDパッケージ一式　*USA*
CL: Pinebender/ Ohio Gold Records　CD, AD, D: Andy Mueller　DF: Ohio Girl Design

CD Cover & Booklet CDジャケット　*Germany*
CL: Christoph Soldan (Pianist)　CD: Kirsten Dietz　AD, D: Felix Widmaier　DF: strichpunkt agentur fur visuelle kommunikation gmbh

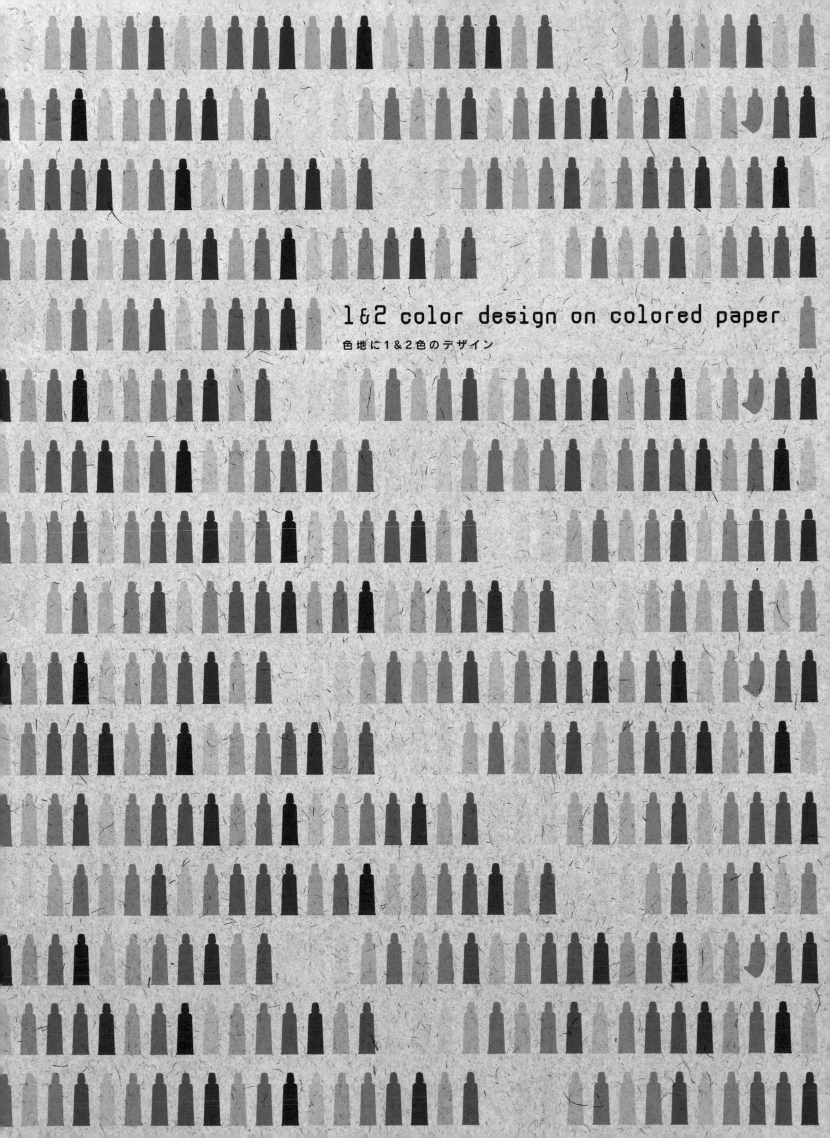

1&2 color design on colored paper
色地に1&2色のデザイン

JAZZ IN WILLISAU
SAMSTAG, 12. OKTOBER 02
20.00 UHR IM NEUEN
CLUB FOROOM / WELLIS AG
CHRISTY DORAN'S
NEW BAG
CHRISTY DORAN G
BRUNO AMSTAD VOICE
HANS PETER PFAMATTER P
FABIAN KURATLI DR, PERC
WOLFGANG ZWIAUER E-B
CD-TAUFE UND
CLUB OPENING

  M Process Black
White

Concert Poster コンサートポスター   *Switzerland*
CL: Jazz in Willisau   AD, D, P: Niklaus Troxler   DF: Niklaus Troxler Design

色地に1＆2色の
デザイン | 1&2 color design
on colored paper | 181

PANTONE 647 U
PANTONE Orange 021 U

Poster アートギャラリーポスター *USA*
CL: Artspace AD, D: Noah Scalin DF: ARF Design

PANTONE 395 U
PANTONE 191 U

Byproduct Catalog 美術展示会カタログ *USA*
CL: Southern Exposure   AD, D: Efrat Rafaeli   DF: Efrat Rafaeli Design

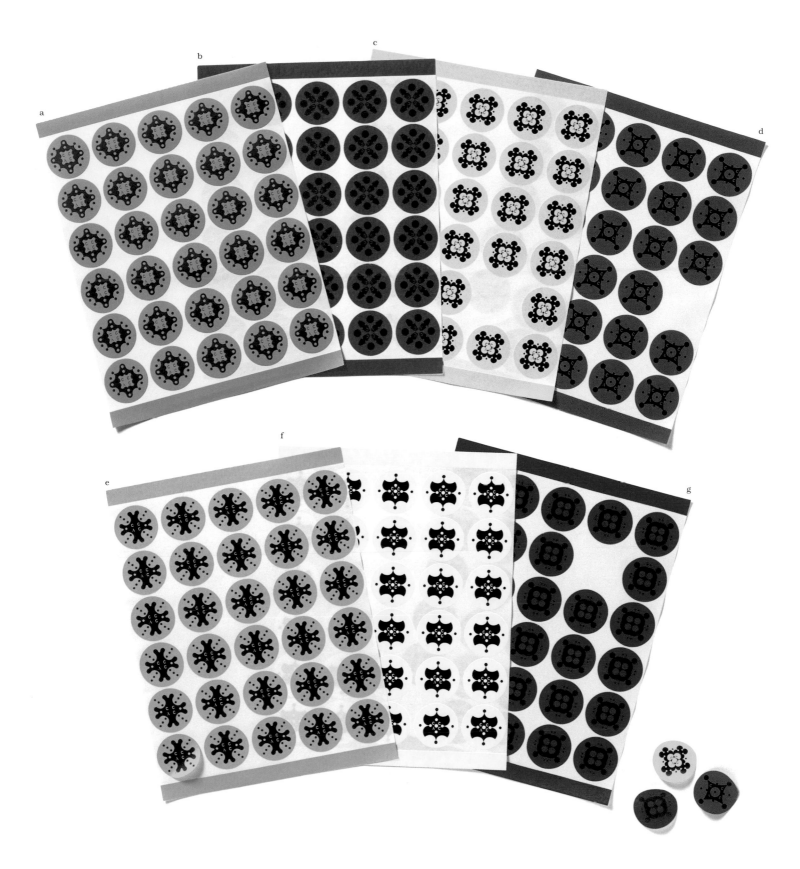

Sheets of Stickers 大学使用のシール *USA*
CL: California College of Arts and Crafts   AD: Bob Aufuldish   D: Richard Chang   DF: Aufuldish & Warinner

PANTONE 308 U

Annual Report 児童施設アニュアルレポート *USA*
CL: Santa Fe Children's Museum   AD, D: Brian Hurshman   P: Scott Plunket   DF: Cisneros Design Inc.

a-2

a-1

b-2

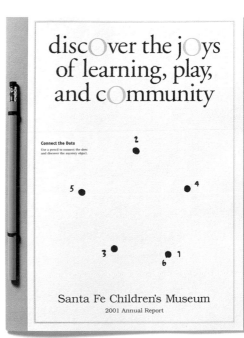

b-1

a-1		PE	PANTONE 539 U PANTONE 877 U

a-2			PANTONE 539 U

b-1			PANTONE 2765 U PANTONE 578 U

b-2			PANTONE 2765 U

Annual Report 児童施設アニュアルレポート　*USA*
CL: Santa Fe Children's Museum　AD: Brian Hurshman　D: Janine Pearson　P: Scott Plunket　DF: Cisneros Design Inc.

Annual Report 児童施設アニュアルレポート　*USA*
CL: Santa Fe Children's Museum　AD: Brian Hurshman　D: Yvette Jones　P: Scott Plunket　DF: Cisneros Design Inc.

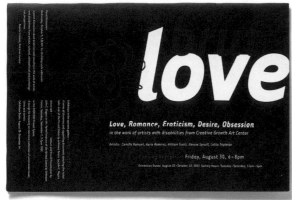

PANTONE 226 U
PANTONE 5395 U

Poster 美術展示会ポスター　*USA*
CL: Southern Exposure　D, I: Efrat Rafaeli　DF: Efrat Rafaeli Design

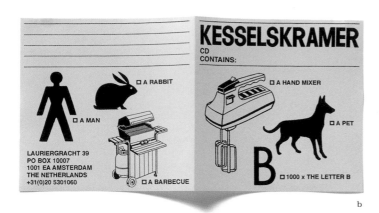

CD & Plastic Bag 広告会社使用CD・バッグ   *The Netherlands*   *a - c
CL: Kessels Kramer   CD: Erik Kessels   AD, P: Krista Rozema   D, I: Anthony Burril   DF: Bless The Artist

Folder アパレル企業イベント用フォルダー   *Italy*   *d
CL: Nike Italy   CD: Barbara Longiardi   AD, D: Alberto Cassani   DF: Matitegiovanotte

a — Process Black
b — Process Black
c — Process Black
d — Process Black / PANTONE 3015 U

a

b

back

  Process Black
PANTONE 138 U

  PANTONE 4975 U
PANTONE 223 U

a

b

Exhibition Direct Mail ギャラリー告知DM   *Japan*
CL: Kei Matsushita Design Room Inc. （有）松下計デザイン室   AD, D: Kei Matsushita 松下計   DF: Kei Matsushita Design Room Inc. （有）松下計デザイン室

Postcard 洋服店ポストカード   *USA*
CL: Standard   CD: Bill Gardner   AD: Brian Miller   D: Luke Bott   DF: Gardner Design

色地に1&2色の
デザイン | **1&2 color design
on colored paper** | 189

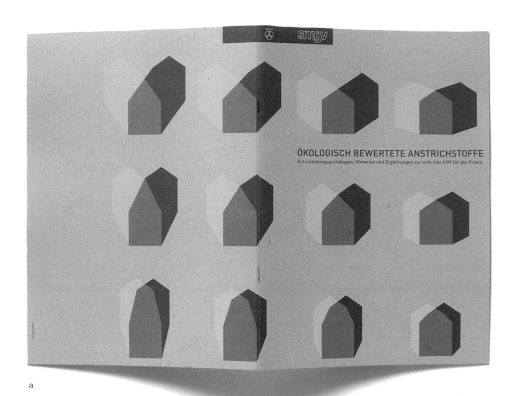

a

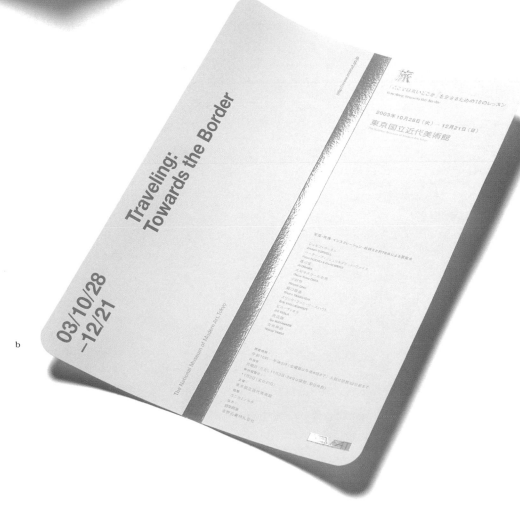

b

a M | PANTONE 576 C
White

b T | DIC-F274 (≒PANTONE 361 C)
Thermography

Brochure, Environmental saftey comparison of paints 協会（画家の集合体）のブローシャー他 *Switzerland*
CL: Schwizerischer Maler -und Gipserunternehmer-Verband smgv AD: Lucia Frey D: Sandro Zorzenone DF: Wild & Frey

Flyer 美術館展覧会チラシ *Japan*
CL, SB: The National Museum of Modern Art Tokyo 東京国立近代美術館 AD, D: Takuya Yamada 山田拓矢 D: Yoko Ariyoshi 有吉陽子 DF: list リスト

  M PANTONE 186 U White

Direct Mail デザイン事務所PR用DM *USA*
CL: Smart Design   DF: Smart Design

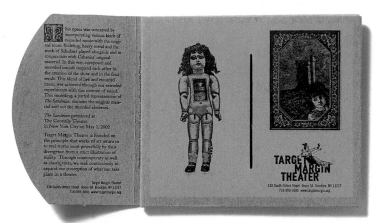

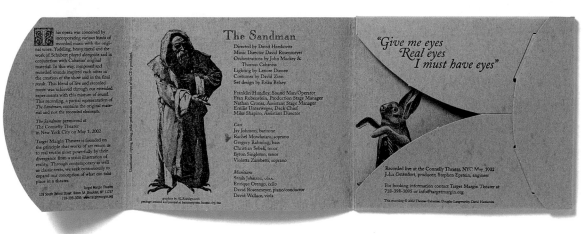

Process Black
PANTONE 5594 U

PE

Process Black
PANTONE 8123 U

CD Cover 劇場制作CDのジャケット   *USA*
CL: Target Margin Theater   AD, D: Noah Scalin   DF: ALR Design

Invitation 劇場案内状   *USA*
CL: Thirteenth Night Theatre Company   AD, D, I: Noah Scalin   DF: ALR Design

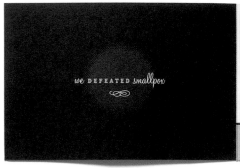

PANTONE 5575 U
PANTONE 4625 U

PANTONE 167 U
PANTONE 385 U

Direct Mail & Brochure 医療会社DM兼ブローシャー *USA*
CL: OHSU   D, I: Karen Wippich, Jon Wippich   CW: Tom Vandel   DF: Dotzero Design

Brochure ブローシャー *USA*
CL: Beaverdale Business Coalition   CD, AD, D, I: John Sayles   D: Som Inthalangsy   DF: Sayles Graphic Design

色地に1＆2色の
デザイン | 1&2 color design
on colored paper | 193

back a front

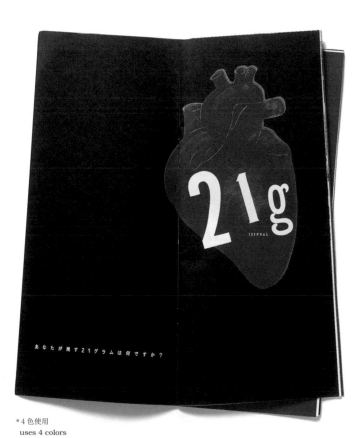

*4色使用
uses 4 colors

b

 M White

  M Process Black
White

a b

Pamphlet 映画「21g」プログラムパンフレット *Japan*
CL, SB: Gaga Communications ギャガ・コミュニケーションズ

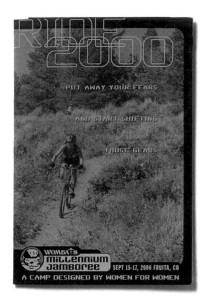

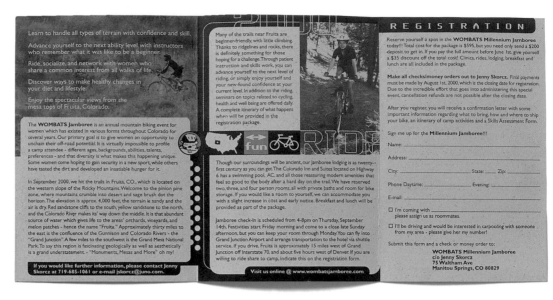

  Process Black

  Process Black
PANTONE Red 032 U

Brochure 自転車クラブ ブローシャー   *USA*
CL: Wombats   AD, D: Sandy Gin   DF: Sandy Gin Design

Leaflet 専門学校リーフレット   *Hong Kong*
CL: Tsun Martial Arts Institute   AD, D: Joseph Leung   DF: Motakding Design

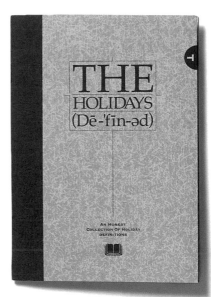

PANTONE 287 U

PANTONE 348 U

Process Black

PANTONE 8922 U

Holiday Card　デザイン事務所グリーティングカード　*USA*
CL: Rickabaugh Graphics　D: Eric Rickabaugh　DF: Rickabaugh Graphics

Invitation　製紙会社展覧会案内状　*USA*
CL: B.W.Wilson　AD, D, P: Noah Scalin　DF: ALR Design

a

*エンボス
Embossing

b

a ⬜ PE PANTONE 877 U

b PE PE PANTONE 877 U
PANTONE 549 U

Brochure パスポートサイズ ブローシャー *Mexico*
CL: Nike   CD, D: Vanessa Eckstein   D: Mariana Contegni   DF: Blok Design

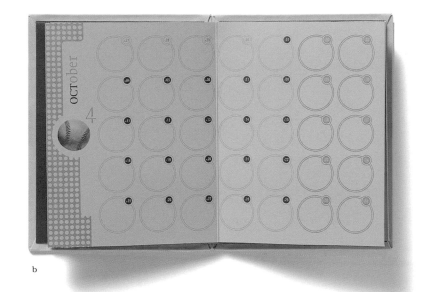

b

a

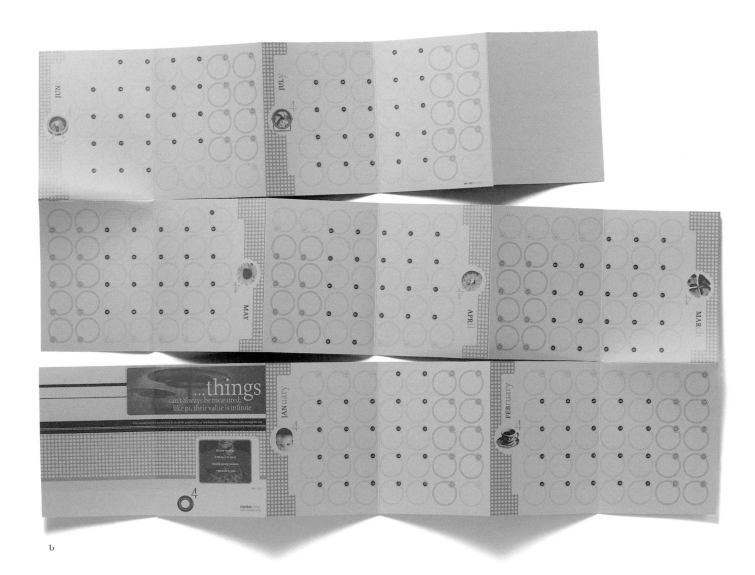

b

a

	H	Silver

	PE	PE	PANTONE 877 U
			PANTONE 8620 U

b

Calender デザイン事務所PR用カレンダー　*Canada*
CL: Riordon Design　CD: Ric Riordon　AD, D: Shirley Riordon　D: Alan Krpan, Amy Montgomery　DF: Riordon Design

a

b

c

a

b

d

Paper Promotion Piece 用紙販促用シート *Switzerland*
CL: Buttenpapierfabrik Gmund GmbH & Co. KG   CD, AD: Heinz Wild   DF: Heinz Wild Design

a | PE | S, PE | S | PANTONE 877 U / PANTONE 375 U
b | PE | S, PE | S | PANTONE 877 U / PANTONE 375 U
c | PE | S, PE | S | PANTONE 877 U / PANTONE 375 U
d | PE | S, PE | S | PANTONE 877 U / PANTONE 375 U

PANTONE 877 U

Wedding Invitation 個人結婚式の招待状 *Germany*
CL: Nicola + Frank Michhoefer   CD, AD, D: Herbert Rohsiepe   DF: graphische formgebung

a-1

absolute pearl   intensive lightening, smoothing, anti-oxidant and oxygenating mask

mask

with pearl powder, procyinidins, licorice, mulberry, bearberry and lemon extracts, salicylic acid, oxygenating factors
use for an immediate illuminating effect, with just one treatment
for a whitening effect, once or twice a week, according to skin type, for at least 2 months
results skin glows - pigmentation irregularities are reduced - oxygen is restored

maschera intensiva ad azione illuminante, schiarente, levigante ed ossigenante

whitening glowing mask
maschera schiarente illuminante

con polvere di perla, acido salicilico, estratti di uva ursina, liquirizia, limone, fattori riossigenanti
uso per un effetto éclat immediato, 10 minuti di posa
per attenuare le macchie e uniformare il colorito, 1 o 2 volte per settimana per almeno due mesi
risultati intensa luminosità del viso - attenuazione delle macchie cutanee - profonda riossigenazione

high performance corrector reducing and aiding in the prevention of dark spots   absolute pearl

with kojic dipalmitate, licorice, mulberry, bearberry extracts, pearl powder
use morning and evening and throughout the day for at least 8 weeks
results dark spots are visibly reduced. skin looks even and flawless

corrector

correttore delle macchie cutaneee e degli inestetismi da acne

con kojico dipalmitato, estratto di liquirizia, gelso, uva ursina, polvere di perla
uso sulle macchie mattina e sera e, quando possibile, durante il giorno, per almeno 8 settimane
risultati visibile attenuazione di macchie cutanee e ipercromie localizzate

dark spot deep impact
correttore macchie intensivo

a-2

b

*エンボス
Embossing

c

d

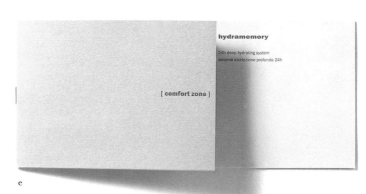

e

Cosmetic Product Cards & Package   化粧品付属カード・化粧品パッケージ   *Italy*
CL: Comfort Zone (Davines)   CD: Natalia Borri   AD: Rachel Wild   DF: The Ad Store Italia

PE

Process Cyan
PANTONE 2757 U

Movietheatre Stationery 劇場ステーショナリー *The Netherlands*
CL: FilmFoyer Tilburg   D: Kees Wagenaars   DF: CASE

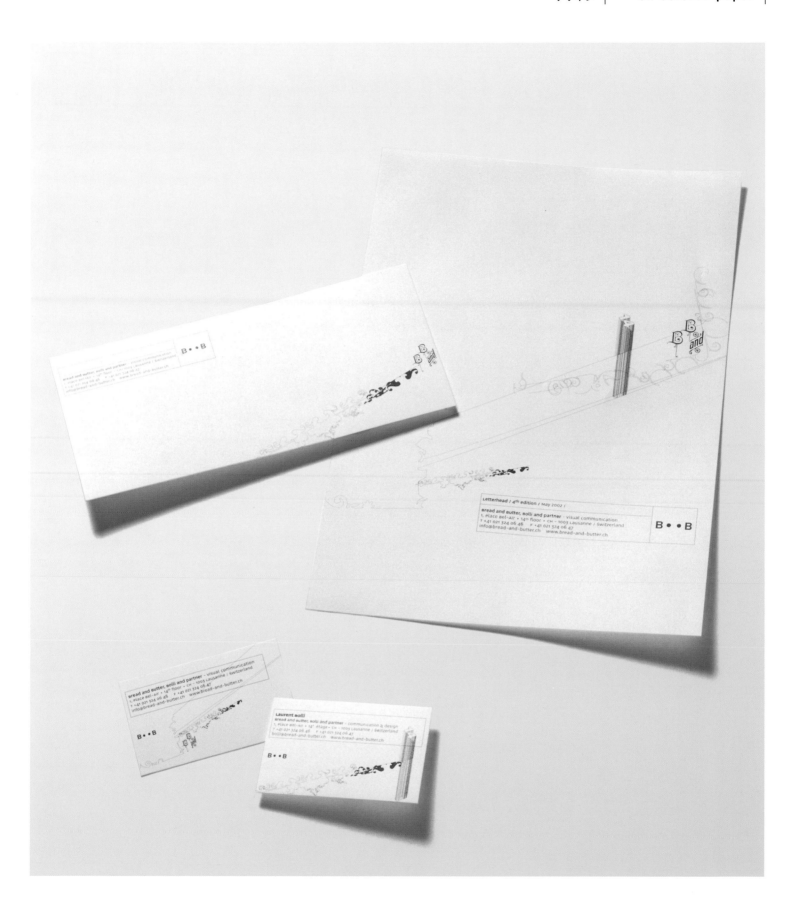

 PANTONE 216 C

Stationery 広告会社ステーショナリー   *Switzerland*
CL: Bread and Butter   CD, AD, D: Cristiana Bolli Freitas   I: Laurent Bolli   DF: Bread and Butter

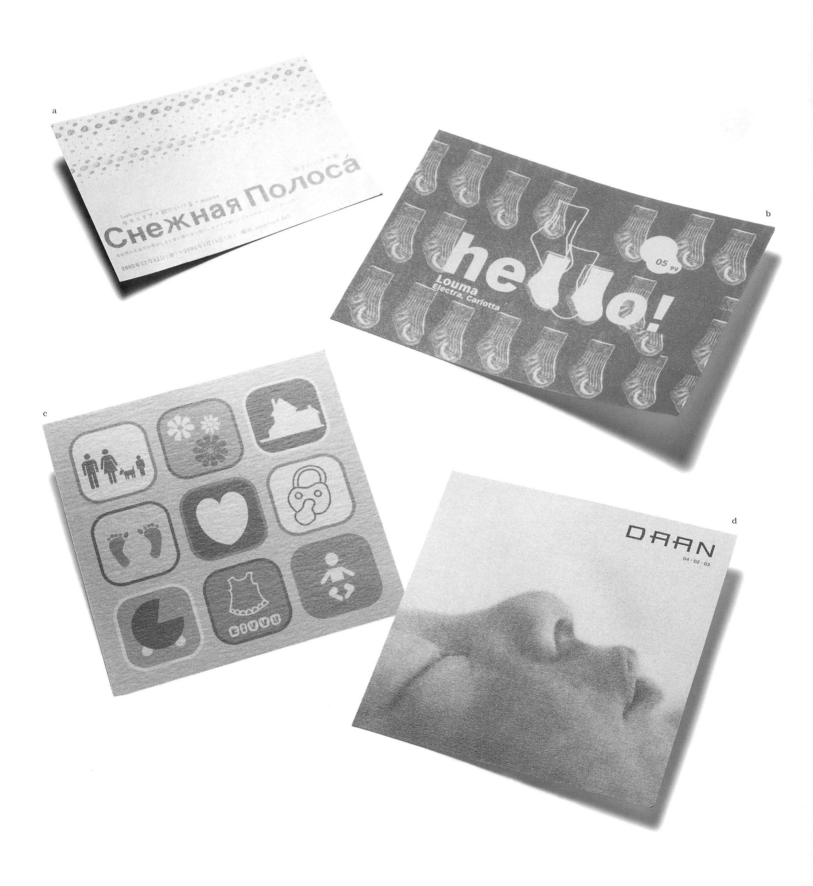

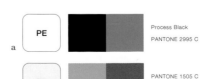

Direct mail 展覧会告知DM　*Japan*　*a
CL: standard deli　ゆきのパフサ展　CD, AD, D: Yurio Seki　セキユリヲ

Baby Greeting Card 個人使用カード　*Switzerland*　*b
CL: Private　CD, AD, D: Cristina Bolli Freitas　I: Laurent Bolli　DF: Bread and Butter

Birth Announcement 個人・出産のお知らせハガキ　*The Netherlands*　*c
CL: KOS　D: Kees Wagenaars　P: Arnoud Kos　DF: CASE

Birth Announcement 個人・出産のお知らせハガキ　*The Netherlands*　*d
CL: Van Gastel/ Wessels　D: Kees Wagenaars　DF: CASE

a　PE　　Process Black　PANTONE 2995 C

b　PE　F　PANTONE 806 U

c　PE　　PANTONE 1505 C　PANTONE 2582 C

d　PE　　PANTONE 2623 C

PE   PANTONE 213 U

Announcement 美術展示会DM *USA*
CL: Southern Exposure D: Efrat Rafaeli DF: Efrat Rafaeli Design

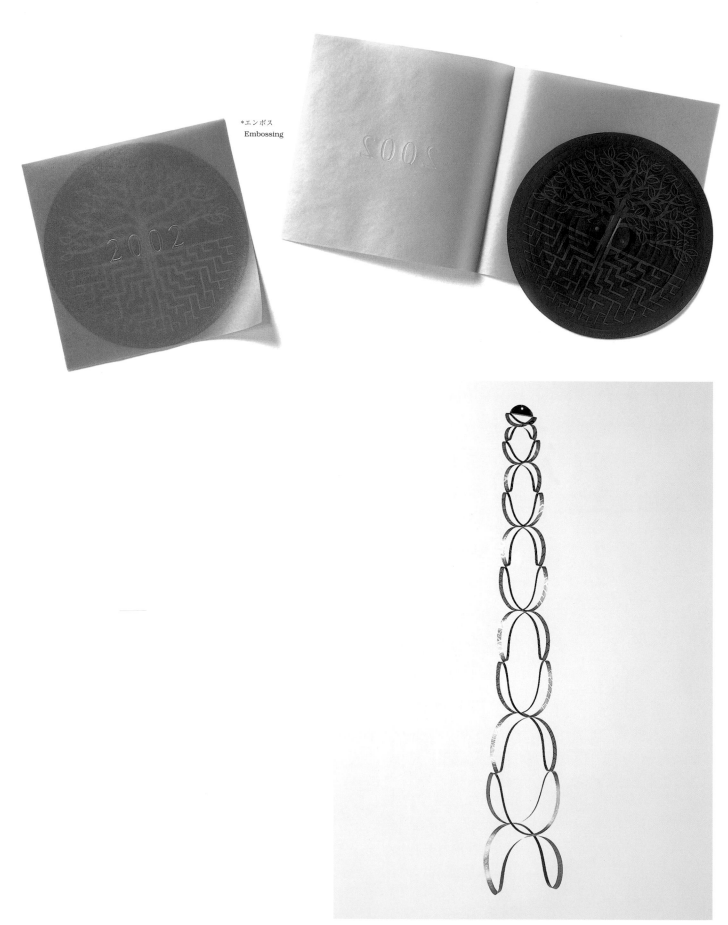

*エンボス
Embossing

*カードはつりさげられることによって、クリスマスの飾りになる。
Card can be hanged as a Christmas decoration.

 PE PANTONE 874 C

Greeting Card 広告会社グリーティング・カード *France*
CL: Actia   CD: Anne-Lise Dermenghem

Special Articles vol.2
+ Submittor's Index

特集：2色印刷のシュミレーション + 出品者データ

特集：2色印刷のシュミレーション

Special Articles on Simulations of Two Colored Printing

制作コストを下げるために印刷色数を下げるということが、必ずしもデザインの幅を狭くするするというわけでない。4色による印刷では表現しにくい微妙な色を、印刷インクを特定して（特色の使用）表わす手法もよく用いられる。また特色2色の掛け合わせでしか生まれない色を使ってデザインすることで、特別な個性を造り出すことも可能だ。その他にブラック（スミ）によるモノクロームを基調に、効果的なワンポイントカラーとして特色を使う2色デザインも、よく使われる手法だ。ここでは、様々な2色印刷の表現目標と掲載された作品をシュミレーション比較して、多くのデザイン手法を紹介していく。

2色印刷の表現目標と掲載作品シュミレーション

1 インパクトのある2色印刷（例：ポスター）

まず重要となるのが色の選択。例えば、特色＋プロセスブラックの場合、特色を使用するということは、掛け合わせにはない、はっきりとした色が使用できるということであり、それを利点として使うことができる。その色の持つ強さ（イメージ）を全面に打ち出すようなデザインが必要となる。同時に、タイポフェイスにも大きな特徴を持たせることで、他にはない個性をつくり出すことが重要。ただ、あまり多種のフォントを使用すると、紙面の持つ2色印刷独特の集中力が失われ、力強さ（イメージ）を弱めることになってしまう。1種のタイポフェイスに個性を持たせる方が作品の独自性が増す。また、大きな画面で見せるポスターのデザインにおいては、それが平面的にならないよう、立体的に見せる仕掛けを考えたい。ビジュアルそのものが立体的な陰影の濃いものであれば、それを生かすか、依存することができる。それ以外の場合は個性的な立体的なタイプフェイスを使用することで、イメージを一変することができる。
（P51, P56）

Lowering the print ink figure to cut down the cost, does not also mean narrowing the possibilities of design. By choosing a specific color, it can become a very useful way for expressing the detail color image. And by mixing two specific colors, a new original color can be made and used in your design. There is also a way of using a black ink as a main image and also using a different color as an effective one point color. These are some of the ways we often see in two colored print techniques. In this article, we will look at the some of two colored print techniques by using the work simulation.

Purpose of Two Colored Printing and Simulations.

1. Two Colored Printing with Impact (ex. Poster)

Choosing the color to use will be the most important task. For example, when using Process Black and one other color, it will be important to use the vivid color and it's image as an advantage. Design must be strong enough to express the color image fully. Other task will be choosing the typography that can create an originality into the work. It will be safe not to use so many different types of typography. This can weaken the image of color.
（P51, P56）

▲ P51

▲ P55

2. Expressing High Class and Dignity in Design (ex. Brochure)

The most important thing in creating company brochure is deciding the fundamental policy of the company itself. But leaving that a side, it is often requested of company brochure design to express high class and dignity.The chosen basic color is usually the corporate image color. For choosing the other color, it is very important to know that person can feel elegant image towards colors that look a like. So if not for a particular case, it is safe to choose a color that has the same image. The basic and important element of design will be the Composure, Stability, and Refined Image. But you also need to express the strong image as well. The accent in space between the typography and illustration and pictures will make that possible. Using a white colored (using the color of paper) font on color and pictures are one example. Not using so many font, and the balance of typography are also key elements.
（P44, 45）

3. Expressing the Image of Full Color (ex. Poster, Brochure)

Choosing the Color will be the most important task. Choosing colors that look a like can be used to express the color depth. Look a like colors can be use to express the color that almost resembles 4 colored print. This shows that to create the many visual side of color, farest colors are not the right match. Typography are often shown by using the white color of the paper. This also can be thought as one color. It is important to use the typography that can leave an impact to the whole design image.
（P20, 24）

2　高級感・品格の演出 （例：会社案内）

企業の誠実な姿勢を表わすための会社案内の制作には、その会社姿勢そのものを論じることからが必要であるが、デザインとしては高級感・品格を表現することを求められることがよくある。基調になる色については、コーポレットカラーがある場合にはその色に近い色を考える。暖色系、寒色系、中間色系の方向性と、特色2色の傾向を絞っていくのだが、あまり多くの色を感じさせない方が上品なイメージを感じさせることが多い。次の段階となる、写真と文字のボリューム、配色と基本的なレイアウトのフォーマットを決めるときには、2色印刷を考慮しての基調色が重要となる。落ち着いた雰囲気、安定感、洗練されたイメージをつくり出していくのが必要となる。ただ、上品さというと落ち着いたデザインになりがちだが、誌面には緊張感と迫力も持たせる必要もある。それにはコントラストをつけることが大事になってくる。文字組みの中に写真スペースを組み込むアクセントを付けたり、ベタ色の範囲を大きく取り、その中に白抜き文字を配列する方法などがある。ただこのようなケースでは、色の選択以外にも書体の選択と文字組みの密度の計算が非常に重要となってくる。多くのフォントを使用しない、バランスの取れた、すっきりとした文字組みの使用が大切。行間を詰め過ぎず、美しい行間を意識する必要もある。ただ、個性的なデザインもうるさくならないように注意して使用すれば効果的になる。
（P44, 45）

3　フルカラーを思わせるグラデーションの利用 （例：ポスター、ブローシャー）

色の選択。同系の色の選択も色の深みを表現するには有効な手法である。色相環の90度に位置する関係の2色など、近い色の組み合せで、フルカラーに近い色の深みを表現することができる。多彩な色を再現するのは必ずしも正反対の色の組み合せだけではないということ。文字要素などは、色を使うわけにはいかない場合が多いので、白抜きを活用するのがよい。これも「カラー」と考えられることできる。その場合は、インパクトを残す上でも、書体の種類・サイズ等は際立ったものを使用するのがよいと考えられる。文字、タイプフェイスのデザインで全体に引き締まった印象を与えることも重要となってくる。
（P20, 24）

▲ P44

▲ P45

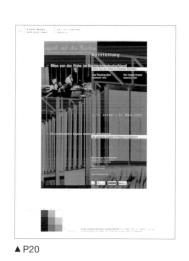

▲ P20

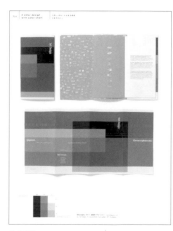

▲ P24

4　プラス1色のアクセント（例：ブローシャー他）

このような場合、基調の色はスミ（プロセス・ブラック）が多いが、スミ色に近い特色の利用も多いだろう。ただ、どのような色を使用するにおいても、ほとんどを単色でデザインするつもりで、基調の色を選択することになる。アクセント用の特色は使用分量は極端に少ないが、それだけに選択された色が作品のシンボルカラーのようにとらえられる。つまりこの特色の選択が重要となってくる。文字を使用する場合にも、書体の選択、文字のレイアウトがとても重要となる。作品の内容が説明なく、書体のイメージから了解されなければいけないのである。そのためオリジナルのタイプフェイス等を利用するのが効果的となる。
（P104, 198）

5　2色で感じさせる楽しい雰囲気（例：ブックレット）

楽しい雰囲気を感じさせるためには、多彩な色づかい、カラフルな印象をつくり出す必要がある。そのため色の選択では、掛け合わせで多彩な色を生み出すことのでできる組み合せの特色2色を使用することになる。特色の単独の階調で異なった色を感じさせ、さらに掛け合わせのバリエーションで様々な色を再現していくことになる。また、用紙の色、とくに白い用紙を用いることが多いが、その白を効果的に使用すると、多彩な色が一層に映えることになる。イラストや写真でいろいろな色を再現するので、文字は補充的な形でデザインした方が成功する。文字に大きな比重を持たせると、カラフルな印象にならずに、重く感じてしまう。
（P12, 13）

4. Using Color as an Accent (ex. Brochure, etc.)

In these cases, the main color is often process black, but what ever color you choose, it is important to think and imagine that you are using only one color for design. Although the other color will be used only for a little amount, you need to think that this color will be a some kind of symbol color for the entire design. It means that choosing this accent color will be the most important task. If this color will be a typography, it's font kind and layout in design will be important also. Original Typography can become very effective.
（P104, 198）

5. Creating a Colorful Fun Image (ex. Booklet)

To create a fun image using a two colored printing, you need to create an image of colorfulness. So in choosing the colors, two mixable colors must be chosen. By using the color steps of one color and the mix of two colors, different variation of colors can be expressed. Also the white color of white paper can be used effectively. This white color can power up the effect of other colors being used. This all can be visualize by the illustration or the pictures in the design, so the typography is placed as a sub-character in the design to keep the whole image not to become so heavy.
（P12, 13）

▲ P104

▲ P198

▲ P12

▲ P13

6. Effective ways of using Silver (ex. Poster)

One of the most particular effect that silver color can give is the impression that differs from all of the other colors. The cool and steel like image can give the same image into the design. It can also give the other color more stand out performance of it's originality. For example, the base color of white paper can stand out as the third color by using silver. (P58, 69)

7. Variation of Colors (ex. CD Cover)

The effect of making different types of two colored designs can be more than you can imagine. It will use the same design, but must look different enough by using the change of colors. The way of choosing the color will begin by selecting the main color and the sub-effect color as a change able color. By carefully finding out the exact image difference for each type, sub-color must be picked to fill the needs. (P176, 177)

6 効果的なシルバー色の利用 （例：ポスター）

シルバーの効果は、色の違いにはない印象をつくることができる点。冷たい金属的なイメージでクールな印象を与えるデザイン。沈んだ明度で、対照的に他の色を目立たせるという補助的な機能。また証明が消えたようなニュートラルな雰囲気をつくって、他の色を際立たせる効果等がある。例として、シルバー、特色、そして白抜きの3色（白抜きを「第三のカラー」として使用）によって目立つ色を白抜きにするというデザイン効果を果たすことができる。これをシルバー以外で試みようとした場合、デザインの効果力が失われてしまうことが想像できる。（P58, 69）

7 バリエーションの面白さ （例：CDジャケット）

同じビジュアル素材で異なったイメージを換起する場合でも2色印刷は想像以上の効果を発揮する。デザイン要素をほとんど変更しないで、別の作品ではないかと思わせる変化を生み出す必要がでてくる。色の選択に関しては、象徴的なカラー（メインカラー）とそれぞれを引き立てるサブカラーとの組み合わせを選択することなる。それぞれの内容を検討しながら、その気分・雰囲気を表現する色を探していく。その中で色選びと色づかいを選択する。（P176, 177）

▲ P58

▲ P69

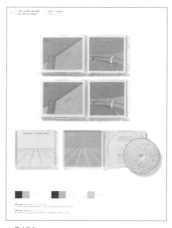
▲ P176

▲ P177

Submittor's Index

出品者データ

> Submittor's Index

出品者データ

限られた色のデザインコレクション
Design Collection with Limited Colors

デザイン Design
柴 亜季子 Akiko Shiba

ジャケットデザイン Cover Design
シラス ノリユキ Noriyuki Shirasu（カラー / Color）

撮影 Photographer
藤本邦治 Kuniharu Fujimoto

制作進行コーディネーター Coordinator
岸田麻矢 Maya Kishida

編集・翻訳 Editor & Translator
小澤研太郎 Ken Ozawa

発行人 Publisher
三芳伸吾 Shingo Miyoshi

一部の掲載写真は出品者からご提供いただいたものを使用させていただいております。
We used the submittor's photographs in some pages.

2008年8月5日　初版第1刷発行

印刷・製本　大日本印刷（株）

発行元　ピエ・ブックス
〒170-005 東京都豊島区南大塚2-32-4
編集　Tel: 03-5395-4820 Fax: 03-5395-4821
　　　e-mail: editor@piebooks.com
営業　Tel: 03-5395-4811 Fax: 03-5395-4812
　　　e-mail: sales@piebooks.com

ISBN978-4-89444-712-7 C3070
Printed in Japan

この本の売上の一部は、出品者の方々のご厚意によりユニセフに寄付されます。
Part of the sales of this book will be donated to UNICEF by courtesy of the submittors.

ご協力のお願い
今回の書籍出版にあたり調査をしましたが、最終的に連絡をとることができなかった出品者の方がいらっしゃいます。
どなたか連絡先をご存じの方がいらっしゃいましたら、お手数ですが小社編集部までご一報下さい。

Please help...
Despite exhaustive investigation in preparing this book, these are still some submittors that we have been unable to contact.
We ask anyone who knows how to contact these people to please notify our editorial staff, and thank you in advance for your assistance.